The Complete Quilt Book

The Complete
Quilt Book

MARTINI NEL

HUMAN & ROUSSEAU
Cape Town   Pretoria   Johannesburg

Copyright © 1997 by Martini Nel
First published in 1997 by Human & Rousseau (Pty) Ltd
State House, 3-9 Rose Street, Cape Town
Translation by Ethné Clarke
Photography by Anthony Johnson
and Peter Bouman on the following pages:
1, 32, 105, 112 and 117
Sketches and patterns by Adri Nel
Typography and cover design by Etienne van Duyker
Text electronically prepared in 11 on 12 pt Janson
Colour reproduction by CMYK, Cape Town
Printed and bound by National Book Printers, Drukkery Street,
Goodwood, Western Cape

ISBN 0 7981 3647 2

Contents

Foreword

*E*ver since I can remember I've been interested in sewing. As a child I enjoyed making dolls clothes and as I grew up, I made my own clothes and particularly enjoyed embroidery. Today I enjoy any kind of sewing and I cant stand being idle.

I made my first quilt in 1981 after my sister-in-law Roleen taught me the basic principles of this kind of sewing. I've never looked back and have wanted to spend all my free time doing quilting since then. Eventually I started spending so much time quilting that it became part of my daily routine. I started giving quilting lessons and in 1985 I started writing books on the subject.

In 1991 I took a trip to America to learn more about quilting. I attended various classes and exhibitions and the Great Quilt Festival in Houston, Texas, amongst others. There were also exhibitions in the Napa Valley and San Francisco in California and I was privileged enough to attend an exhibition of the Tallahassee quilters in Tallahassee, Florida. Thereafter I visited the Amish in Lancaster, Pennsylvania and attended a big exhibition of a select group of quilters in New York.

In 1996 I once again travelled to America for various exhibitions. On this occasion I had the opportunity to present a class in quilting (African Mural Quilts) at the New England Quilt Museum in Lowell, Massachusetts and in Tallahassee, Florida I lectured on the subject of quilting. Both were tremendously enjoyable.

When I started quilting, aids such as quilting yarn, marking pens and long, transparent rulers didnt exist. As these became available new techniques developed. Today a rotary cutter, a long ruler and a sewing machine make it possible to complete the top layer of a quilt within a few hours. In the past it took weeks or even months to make the same layer by hand. Today we can choose between a number of different techniques. There is hand appliqué or machine appliqué, the inlay method, the hand joining method and different machine joining methods such as strip piecing, paper-based and folded-over methods. It is therefore up to you to decide how much time you wish to spend on a quilt and to choose a method accordingly.

In the previous century only quilts and clothes were made by joining little pieces of fabric together. Nowadays one can make any number of different articles and gifts such as a wine bag, hot-water bottle covers or a teddy bear using different quilting techniques.

Quilting is growing in popularity worldwide. It is no longer just a way of getting rid of leftover bits of fabric, but is used in many different ways to forge lasting friendships. Accordingly the official emblem of the 1996 Olympic Games in Atlanta was a quilt. It was called A Quilt of Leaves and it was reproduced on all admission tickets. Each participating country also received a gift of two quilts.

With this book I have tried to inspire both beginner and experienced quilters to try out different techniques for quilts and other articles. Beginners can start with an easy project complete with pattern plates and instructions.

Advanced quilters can look to the photographs of original quilts for inspiration and design their own patterns.

Read the instructions for each article carefully before you embark on a project. Beware of getting imperial and metric measurements mixed up. If you start out using the metric system you must stick with it and the same goes for imperial measurements.

Follow the instructions and start working on that family heirloom today. When you've made yourself enough quilts, you can start on quilts or quilted articles for your children, grandchildren, friends and other relatives.

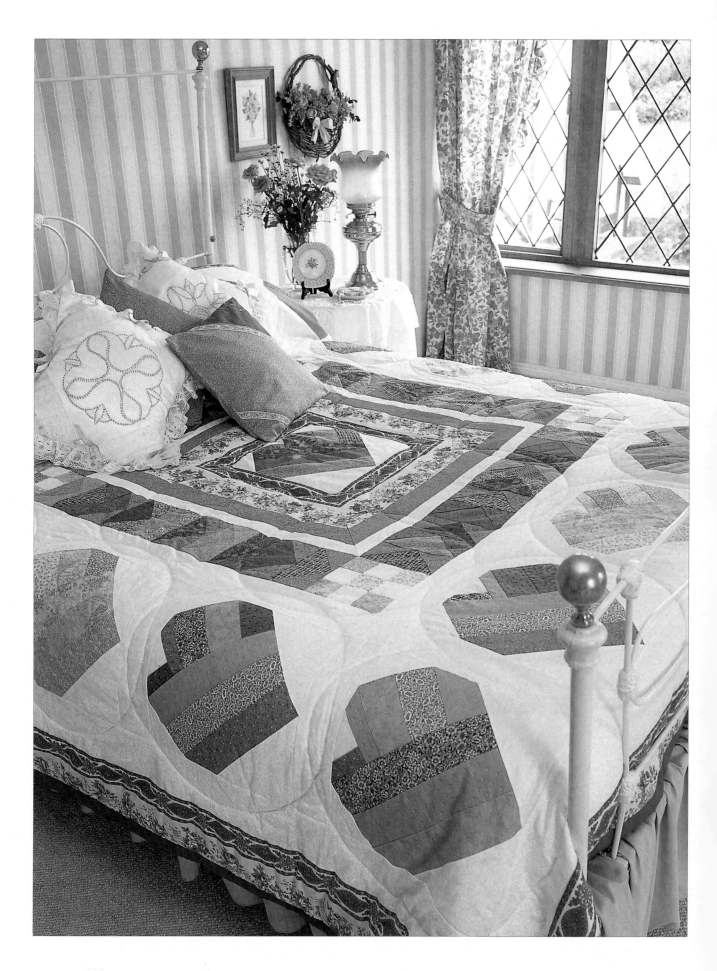

Materials and equipment

Having the right basic equipment at your disposal will fascilitate the making of your article. So do make sure you have all the necessary materials and equipment at hand before you begin a needlework project.

Various handy items are available. For example, a rotary cutter, cutting block and long ruler will save time when you have to cut many strips of fabric. A rotary cutter cuts cleanly through several layers of fabric at the same time. If you use a long ruler, it will not be necessary to make a cutting line before you begin cutting.

Although many new tools have appeared on the market recently, it is not necessary to buy all of them. First examine an item carefully to establish whether it is worth buying, or you may end up with an expensive item which you never use.

Below is a list of essential materials and equipment required for making quilted articles.

Needles

A large variety of needles are available. Making sure you buy the right needles for the specific needlework project will save you a lot of frustration.

Use *sharp-pointed needles* (no thicker than no. 8) for joining patches and pieces. A thin needle penetrates the layers of fabric more easily and will speed up your work. Make sure the needle's eye is large enough.

Special *quilting needles* (called betweens) are best for quilting. Use nos. 8 to 12, depending on your preference.

Machine needles must be replaced frequently to prevent poor quality stitching and tension. I prefer no. 80 Universal needles.

Pins

Pins are more important than most people think. Use long, smooth pins that do not rust. They should be thin enough not to leave holes in the fabric, especially when you are using finely woven fabric.

Thread

The right thread for a specific technique and article is essential.

A *hundred per cent mercerised cotton thread* that blends with the colour scheme of the fabric is suitable for joining patches and for appliqué.

I prefer using less expensive *basting thread*. Do not use a very dark basting thread on light-coloured fabric since it could leave marks.

Special *quilting thread* is best for quilting. It is very strong and does not tangle so easily. It makes a big difference in quilting. The stitch is more visible because the thread is slightly thicker than ordinary thread. Choose the shade of the quilting thread with care. It may be the same shade as the article, a contrasting shade, or various shades that blend with the article for a special effect.

Embroidery thread and *embroidery wool* may be used for embroidering detail on a motif, or for finishing seams such as blanket-stitched appliqué.

Scissors

An inexpensive *pair of scissors* is suitable for cutting the parts of a pattern and paper. This is also the only pair of scissors your husband or children may borrow!

A good pair of *long-bladed needlework scissors* is a good investment. Use this pair exclusively for cutting fabric. There is no greater frustration than battling with blunt scissors when you are quilting.

A pair of *small, sharp-pointed scissors* is very handy for snipping threads, especially when quilting.

Rotary cutter

A rotary cutter simplifies the task of cutting through several strips of fabric at the same time. It is preferable to buy the larger rotary cutter which can cut through several layers of fabric at the same time and which does not easily become blunt. Always make sure there are no pins in the way of the rotary cutter when cutting, since pins can damage the blade irreparably.

Cutting board

A cutting board is essential for protecting the work surface when you are using a rotary cutter. Never test the rotary cutter blade on any other surface, such as wood, since you could damage both the blade and the surface.

Measuring tools

A variety of rulers are available.

An *ordinary ruler* is suitable for simple tasks such as tracing patterns onto graph paper.

A special *long ruler* (60 cm/24 in.) is obtainable at some craft shops. The ruler is also marked with a 45-degree angle. I regard it as an essential item for cutting strips of fabric. Once you have worked with a long ruler you will never want to be without one.

Long strips of plastic of various widths can be obtained from a plastics dealer, if you cannot find a long ruler. Widths used are generally 2½ cm (1 in.), 3 cm (2¼ in.), 5 cm (2 in.), 7 cm (2¾ in.) and 10 cm (4 in.).

A *6 mm (¼ in.) wide guide strip* (quilter's quarter) for adding seam allowances is also available.

Thimble

There are many kinds of thimbles.

You will need two thimbles, especially for quilting. One thimble is for the middle finger of the right hand and one for the index of the left hand.

Those who cannot work with a normal thimble should try a *leather thimble*. (Cut off the finger of an old leather glove if leather thimbles are unobtainable.)

Needleworkers with long nails can use a *special thimble* with an opening at the top.

Soft pencil

A sharp, soft pencil is necessary for tracing lines around templates onto fabric.

Water-soluble pen

A special blue water-soluble pen is particularly handy for marking quilting patterns. Never iron over the pen lines and rinse the article in cold water, otherwise the ink may stain it. First test the pen on a piece of fabric to check that it does not spread and that it washes out.

Masking tape

Different widths of masking tape are used for marking quilting patterns. The narrowest masking tape (6 mm/¼ in. wide) is particularly suitable for marking straight lines with echo and outline quilting.

A broader masking tape, for example 2,5 cm (1 in.) wide, may be used for marking patterns for background quilting. The broadest masking tape (5 cm/2 in.) is suitable for cutting out motifs, for example leaves and hearts. You paste it onto the article and quilt around the masking tape. It can be peeled off and used again.

Glue

A glue stick (Pritt) is necessary for pasting paper onto the plastic of X-ray films.

Quilting frames and hoops

An embroidery or a quilting frame may be used for quilting small and large articles. When quilting a large article, you simply move the frame to the next part of the quilt.

Batting

Batting comes in different thicknesses. The quality differs also.

I prefer a thinner batting for my quilts. It is easier to quilt neatly if your batting is not too thick.

Some kinds of batting eventually tend to form lint on the outside of the article. This is an annoying problem quilters are faced with.

In some countries batting is manufactured according to strict specifications concerning quality and thickness. Unfortunately, we are still in a position where we have to be satisfied with whatever quality we can get. If there is a craft shop close to you that imports batting, I would recommend that you buy your batting from them. Then you will be assured of good quality.

Polyester

Polyester filling is used for stuffing various articles, such as teddy bears and cushions. It is completely washable.

The choice of fabric plays an important role when making quilted articles.

For patchwork articles, a 100 per cent cotton fabric is best. It washes well, is durable and easy to fold, cut and join. Mixtures of cotton and polyester are suitable too. Choose fabrics with the same characteristics for an article, since washing and use will affect different kinds of fabric differently.

When choosing fabric, take the following into account:
● The fabric must not stretch;
● The fabric must not fray too much;
● The fabric must be colourfast;
● The fabric must not shrink;
● The fabric must not be too thick for the needle to penetrate.

Rinse the fabric beforehand as a precaution. Wash dark colours separately and iron all fabric thoroughly before use.

Choice of fabric colours for a quilt

The success of a quilted article depends largely on the colours of the fabric you choose. With most patterns, the colour value – whether the colour of the fabric is light, medium or dark – will determine the best effect of the pattern. If you are uncertain about whether your fabric colour is light, medium or dark, try photocopying small pieces. The shades will show up clearly on the black-and-white photocopy so that you can decide in which group to classify them.

Generally it is essential to use light and dark colours together in a quilt.

For example, use light, medium and dark shades of pink for a quilt. The Kaleidoscope quilt on page 41 is a splendid example of how effective the use of different shades of colour can be. Consider the shades and tones of your colours before you begin a project.

When choosing colours for a specific article such as a quilt you must decide whether you prefer a warm or cool effect. Warm colours such as red or yellow can make a quilt appear warmer. Cooler colours are blue or green. A combination of warm and cool colours is generally very effective.

Choice of fabric design for a quilt

The different fabrics used for a quilt should never have the same pattern, as this could be very monotonous. You will need fabrics with small motifs such as dots or spots or dainty flowers, as well as fabrics with medium-sized motifs and larger motifs.

If the motifs are dense, it would be more suitable to cut them into smaller patches.

The contrast between the printed motif and the background of a fabric may be too great, for example a white background with dark-blue motifs. It would be much more prominent and often even more difficult to use than a fabric with a dark-blue motif on a blue background.

Fabric with a border pattern is particularly suitable for border strips. The strips for the Hearts quilt on page 82 were cut from such fabric.

Making templates

To make a template, proceed as follows:

If a template at the back of this book is the size you require, trace or photocopy it. Cut out the duplicate pattern and paste it onto thin plastic with a glue stick, for example the plastic from used X-ray films. Cut it out carefully.

Mark all templates so that you do not confuse them later on. Write the name of each template down, and how many of each must be cut out. Write down how many parts the pattern consists of; in this way you will notice immediately if one is lost.

If a template tends to slip on the fabric, paste a small piece of masking tape or fine sandpaper onto the back.

If a template is not the size you require, enlarge or reduce it with a photocopier. Just make sure the photocopier you use enlarges or reduces the pattern accurately, since some photocopiers tend to produce inaccurate copies.

You may also use graph paper to enlarge or reduce a pattern by changing the scale.

Usually seam allowances are not added to templates.

Single-seam method

Place the template on the wrong side of the fabric. Add a seam allowance of 6 mm (¼ in.) around each template. Trace the outlines very accurately onto the fabric with a soft pencil. Be particularly precise when you come to the corners. Proceed until all the pattern pieces have been traced (fig. 1a). Now cut out the patches or pieces – not forgetting to add a seam allowance.

Before joining the pattern pieces, first arrange the pieces until you are satisfied with the pattern and effect. If one of the colours are not quite to your liking, cut other patches. It pays dividends to be meticulous during this stage, otherwise you may well have a finished article which you dislike!

The sequence for joining the pieces requires special attention. Always attempt to join the pieces in units. Then join the units so that they form a block. Do not simply begin with any piece joining the rest one by one. This will take more time and the work will not look neat. First decide on the easiest sequence and continue in that way.

Hand method

Place two pieces together with right sides facing.

Pin the layers of fabric neatly in the corners (fig. 1b). Insert another pin along the stitching line and make sure the two pieces correspond perfectly.

Begin with a double stitch and sew small straight stitches from corner to corner. End with a double stitch.

If the seam is long, sew a small double stitch every few centimetres to strengthen the seam.

Press the seam flat with your fingers. Do not open the seam, rather smooth it towards the darker fabric so that the seam is not visible.

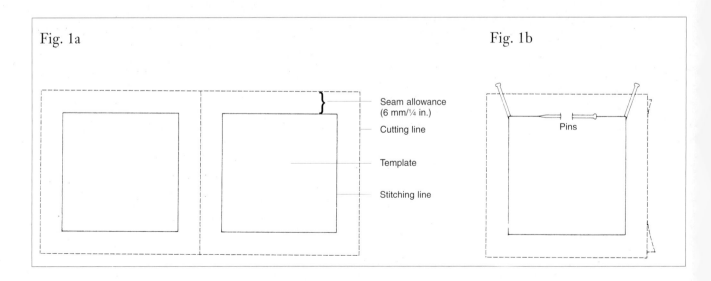

Fig. 1a

Fig. 1b

Seam allowance (6 mm/¼ in.)

Cutting line

Template

Stitching line

Pins

Machine method

Place two pieces together with right sides facing.

Now insert a pin at each corner, making sure the pin penetrates the corners of both layers of fabric. Insert another pin along the stitching line, taking care that the stitching lines correspond. First pin as many pieces as the pattern allows in this way.

Set the machine on a medium stitch length and tension and do not stitch a double stitch at the beginning and end – this may cause the stitches to be too tight and to form creases.

Now stitch the pieces together so that the part at the seam allowance is also stitched. Do not cut the thread after stitching each piece; make a "chain" and do all the cutting at the same time – this saves time. Stitch the pieces together according to the pattern.

If you are sure that you can work accurately, you will not need to trace the outlines of the template with a pencil. However, make sure you cut the seam allowance (for example 6 mm/¼ in.) accurately. Use the presser foot of your machine as a guide and stitch the seam allowance of all the pieces the same width. This can save a great deal of time.

Folded-star method

For this technique, small pieces of fabric are folded to form triangles. Then they are sewn onto the background fabric to form star shapes. The folded triangles may also be used to decorate jackets, bags, other clothing items or quilts. Arrange the triangles to form a motif or form a single row of triangles as a variation.

Cut a circle (or a square if you intend making a square article) to the required size from the background fabric. Always cut this fabric a little larger than the finished article has to be. Mark the centre

by folding the circle in half twice.

Cut four squares from the first fabric for the points of the star. Fold each one double. Fold the two corners at the folded edge to the centre so that the fabric forms a triangle (fig. 2a). The folds must be very accurate and preferably be pressed flat.

Place the triangle on the background fabric with the point in the centre (fig. 2b). Sew the point securely to the background fabric. Check whether the bottom of the triangle is neatly closed and tack close to the raw edge. Sew the other three triangles in the same way, making sure the points meet at the centre.

For the second row you will need eight squares of the same size, but in another colour. Fold as before. Place the triangles over the previous triangles with their centre lines corresponding (fig. 2c). The short sides of the triangles must overlap equally. Sew the points together and tack close to the raw edges of the bases of the triangle.

For a third row, use eight fabric pieces. Place them over the previous star points again (fig. 2d). The folded star is now complete and ready to be finished.

> HINT:
> To ensure that your seam allowance always remains exactly the same when you are stitching, paste a piece of mirror adhesive tape (mounting tape) onto your machine to serve as a guide. Measure the correct distance for the seam allowance from your machine needle and paste the mirror adhesive tape onto the machine. This adhesive tape is thick and serves as a buffer to prevent the fabric from shifting past it.

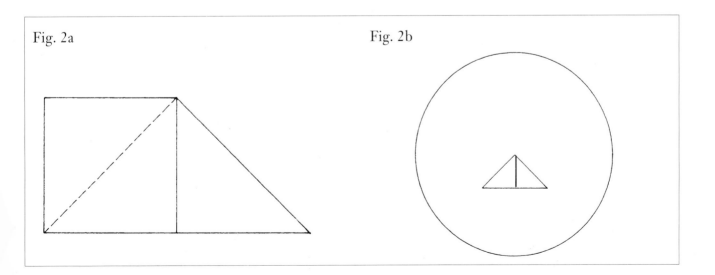

Fig. 2a   Fig. 2b

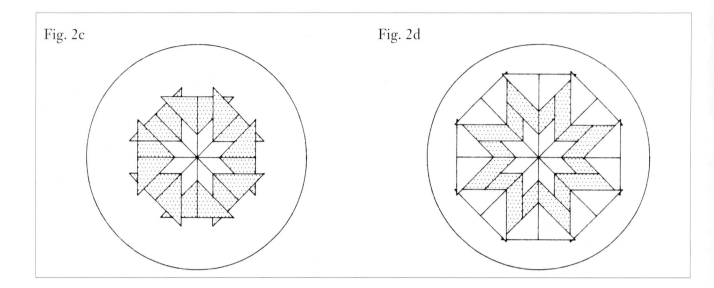

Fig. 2c

Fig. 2d

Inlay method (English patchwork)

With the inlay method, tack paper pieces without seam allowances onto the cut-out fabric pieces with seam allowances. Join with oversewing stitches. Each fabric piece comes on a separate paper piece. To save time, trace the templates onto paper and make photocopies. Or stack a few layers of paper and cut simultaneously, in which case you need only to trace the templates onto the top sheet of paper. Take care not to shift the paper.

Place a paper piece in the centre of a fabric piece.

Pin (fig. 3a).

Begin at one side of a piece. Make a knot in the thread and fold the fabric seam allowance over. Begin about 1 cm (½ in.) from the corner and, using large tacking stitches, tack through the two layers of fabric and the paper (fig. 3b). Fold the fabric around the second side of the paper piece. Tack through all the layers (fig. 3c). Complete all the sides in the same way.

Once all the pieces have been completed, sew them together. Place the pieces two together at a time with right sides facing.

Join with small oversewing stitches (fig. 3d). Begin about 3 mm (⅛ in.) from the corner with a double stitch and sew three small oversewing stitches back to the corner. Make sure the corners are perfectly flush. Do not sew the stitches too far from the edge because it will form a thick join. Now sew oversewing stitches up to the next corner. Sew three stitches back, ending with a double stitch. Snip the thread.

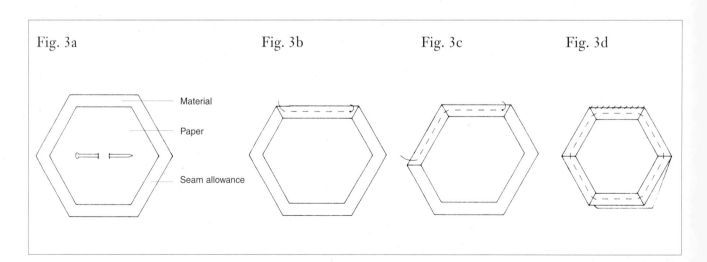

Fig. 3a

Fig. 3b

Fig. 3c

Fig. 3d

Material

Paper

Seam allowance

Join all the pieces according to the pattern. Do not sew the paper as it will be difficult to remove.

Keep the papers in as long as possible to prevent the sides of fabric cut on the bias from stretching.

Log Cabin (folded-over) method

With the Log Cabin or folded-over method, narrow strips of fabric are joined from a point around a centre block. Each strip overlaps with the raw edge of the previous strip. This method is particularly suitable for machine patchwork and is one of the easiest piecing methods.

There are several variations on the Log Cabin method. For example, place the first block in a corner and join the strips to the remaining sides – it will appear as if the pieces are radiating from the corner. This effect can be seen in the green-and-pink Log Cabin quilt on page 80.

The centre square may also be placed so that one part of the pattern is twice the size of the other. The strips of the large part are twice the width of the smaller part.

Additional diamond-shaped pieces may be joined to the strips to form a star, as in the black-and-white Log Cabin Quilt on page 77.

The width of the strips depends on personal taste. A seam allowance of 6 mm (¼ in.) on both sides is generally used. If you cut all the strips first, wait before dividing them up. The centre block may be any size you want. It does not have to be the same width as the strips.

Usually the strips are stitched to paper or a foundation square. This method is discussed below. If you wish, you may leave this out, but then your blocks may not be as accurate when they have been stitched.

The ultimate effect depends to a great extent on the colours you choose. Each square usually consists of a light and a dark part, or of two different colours. All the blocks for a quilt can be made exactly the same by placing all the fabrics in the blocks in the same sequence, or the quilt may be assembled by sewing completely different pieces of scrap fabrics in all the blocks. Keep one half of the square light and the other half dark.

Decide on the sequence in which you intend using the different fabrics.

If you intend making all the blocks exactly the same, with colours running from light to dark, number the fabric to prevent using the wrong fabric, for example no. 1 light, no. 2 dark, and so on. Use a dominant colour for the centre block.

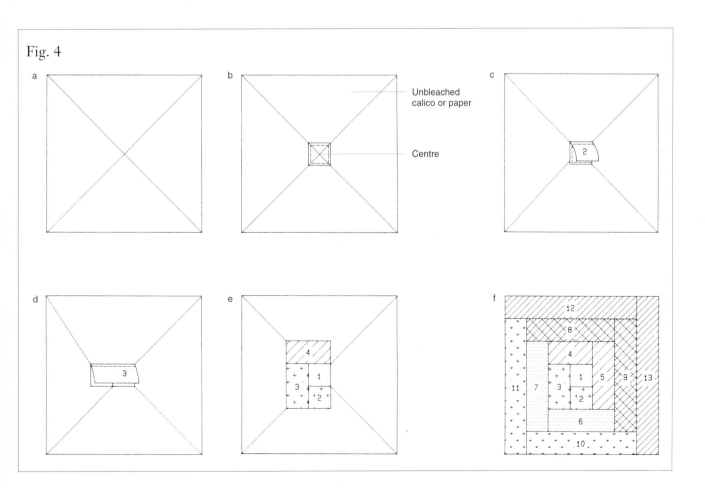

Fig. 4

Fig. 5

a   b   c

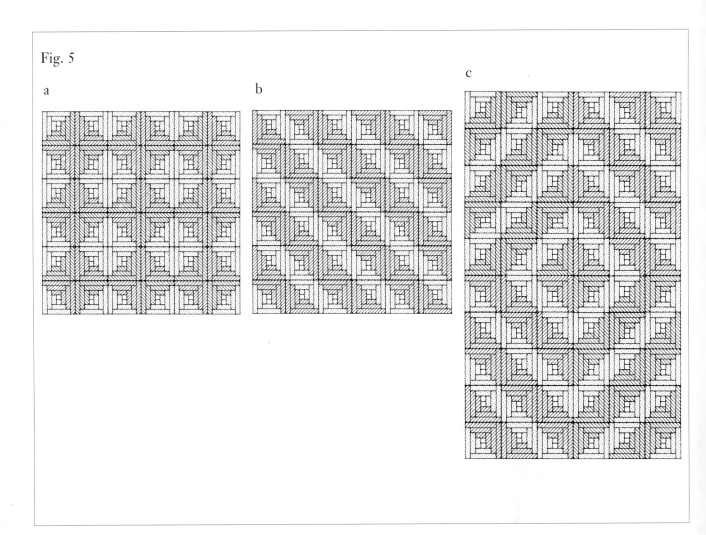

Method

Cut the centre block and the foundation fabric or paper and find the centre of each by folding them on the bias twice. Place the centres over each other with right sides up. Pin and tack (fig. 4a and b).

Begin with the first light-coloured fabric. Place the strip of fabric over the centre block with right sides facing, and pin on one side. Stitch along the seam line with straight stitches (fig. 4c). Trim the excess fabric exactly in line with the edge of the centre block. Fold the piece over, press flat, and pin. Remember always to turn the block in the same direction, so that the part where the next piece is to come lies on top.

Now place the next light-coloured fabric over the previous two pieces with right sides facing and stitch. Trim any excess fabric as before (fig. 4d).

Now stitch the first dark-coloured fabric (fig. 4e). Follow the diagram and complete the block (fig. 4f). When all the blocks have been completed, join them. The effect is determined by the placing of the blocks, therefore it is better to play around with the layout first before joining them (fig. 5).

Strip piecing method

Fabric strips are pieced, cut into sections and then pieced again in long or diagonal strips.

The strips may be any length or width and consist of two or more colours. They are all stitched together with the same seam allowance.

The seam allowance is normally 6 mm (¼ in.) or the width of the machine presser foot.

When using a pattern where the seam allowance has already been included in the cut strips, make sure that your machine presser foot corresponds with the seam allowance, or make provision for a broader seam allowance.

Use a cutting board, rotary cutter and long ruler to facilitate the cutting of the strips. With a sharp rotary cutter you can cut about four layers of fabric at a time. Fold your fabric in half so that it is not so wide when you want to cut it.

Place the fabric on the cutting board and hold the ruler in position with your left hand. Push the rotary cutter away from yourself while holding it against the ruler and pressing down. It must be done with one long sweeping movement to avoid uneven cutting. Always take care not to pass the rotary cutter over pins because this will damage the blade.

Place the strips of fabric two at a time over the length with right sides facing and stitch. Each time, add another strip in the sequence you prefer. Press the seams to one side – preferably towards the darker side of the fabric (fig. 6). Divide the strips into the required widths and join as you wish.

Figure 7 illustrates how a simple four-patch is made. It consists of two strips of different fabric stitched together. The strips are subdivided into small strips which are the same width as the long strips. The small strips are joined so that the different colours are opposite each other.

Figure 8 illustrates how a simple nine-patch is made.

Three strips are joined, for example two light-coloured strips on the outside and one dark-coloured strip in the centre. Another three strips are joined, for example two dark-coloured strips on the outside and one light-coloured strip in the centre. Cut the strips into smaller strips which are the same width as the long strips. Join to form a chequered effect.

Where possible, always try to form a chain when joining strips of fabric (fig. 11), cutting them afterwards.

Follow the diagrams for making different patterns (fig. 9 and 10).

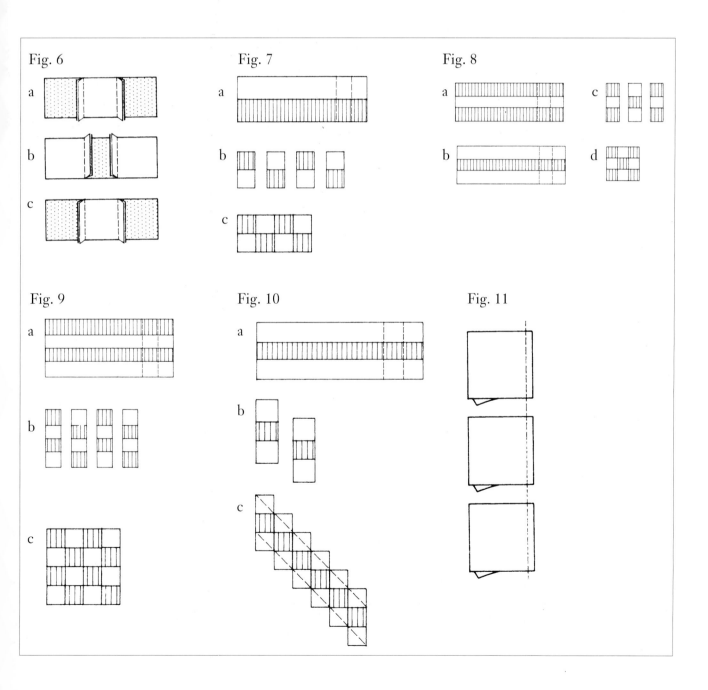

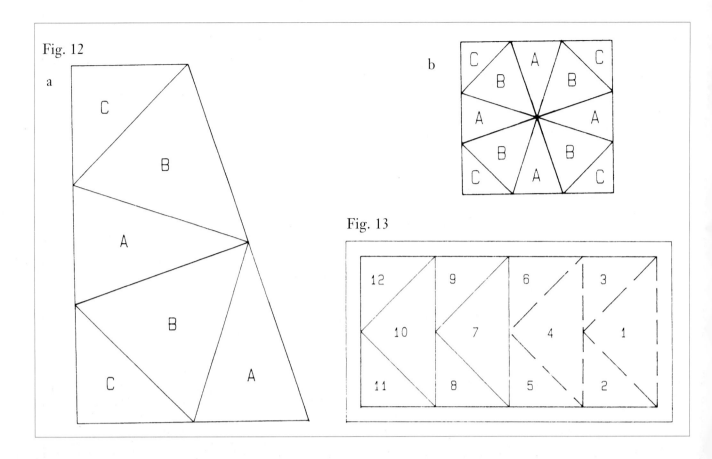

Fig. 12

a

b

Fig. 13

Paper-based machine patchwork

I sometimes call the paper-based method Jolena's method, since Jolena van Rooyen introduced it to many people. Although the method is not suitable for all patterns, it is one of the most accurate forms of machine patchwork.

The pattern is traced onto a sheet of paper (for example the kaleidoscope pattern) and the same number of photocopies are made as the number of blocks.

One of the most important rules with this method is that the raw edge of the first piece is always covered by the next piece. For this reason you cannot stitch the entire block of a kaleidoscope design on one sheet of paper. It will be difficult to cover all the raw edges in the centre. Therefore the pattern is cut in half (fig. 12).

The next rule to remember is that the paper with the lines on face towards you and the fabric is at the bottom of the paper. This means that you see only the pattern lines on the photocopy and not the fabric while you stitch. These are the exact stitching lines.

Proceed stitching as follows:

Cut the pattern pieces with a broader seam allowance than usual. Place the first piece (A) in position on the back of the paper where an A-piece must come. Pin.

Place the next piece (B) over the A-piece with right sides facing and the seam line corresponding. Pin. Make sure that it covers the entire area (B). Stitch exactly along the stitching line. Press the piece back so that it lies flat.

You will find that you frequently have to press the pieces to make them lie flat.

Now stitch the next A-piece and then the next B-piece. Stitch the two corners (C) together. One half of the block is now complete.

Complete the other half in the same way.

Place the two halves together with right sides facing and stitch.

One of the easiest patterns for practising this method is the Flying Geese pattern consisting of three triangles forming a rectangle. Place the large fabric triangle on the wrong side of the paper. Sew the first small triangle to the other side seam and fold over. Now sew the next large triangle over the raw edge of the two small triangles and repeat the entire process until the pattern on the photocopy is complete (fig. 13). Repeat the process with the next photocopy and join the two. In this way you can make long strips where the pattern is repeated.

Once you have mastered this method, you will use it often for making different patterns.

Appliqué has been known from the earliest times. All the different forms of appliqué are used for making quilts. It involves stitching small pieces of fabric onto a background fabric to form a design. This may be done by hand or with a machine, and both forms are briefly discussed.

Virtually any picture or design can be adjusted to serve as an appliqué pattern. Use a photocopier or graph paper to enlarge or reduce a pattern. Each pattern piece of an appliqué pattern is used as a template. Remember, however, to place the top side of a template (in other words, the side on which you have written) on the wrong side of the fabric, otherwise you will have a mirror image of the original pattern.

A pattern is usually composed of several templates, for example six or seven leaves will form a flower. The broderie perse method is different, however. A motif is cut out from print fabric (for example glazed chintz) and stitched directly onto the background.

Machine method

Wonder-Under is recommended for this method. (Wonder-Under is a registered tradename.) You may find a similar iron-on material at your dealer with a different name. It is almost the same as iron-on interfacing, with the important difference that it has glue on both sides. Wonder-Under has paper on one side and the other side is slightly shiny. Iron the Wonder-Under onto the fabric, with the shiny side on the wrong side of the fabric. Remove the paper and iron the fabric onto the background fabric.

Enlarge the design if necessary and trace the pattern onto the shiny side of the Wonder-Under, or iron-on interfacing, if the former is not obtainable. Do not add seam allowances, except where one part is overlapped by another. Cut out the pattern pieces and iron them onto the wrong side of the different fabrics. Cut out the fabric pieces.

Iron the first pattern piece in position. (If using ordinary iron-on interfacing, you will have to tack it onto the background fabric because there is no glue on the back of this interfacing.) Now stitch the pattern piece using a fine zigzag stitch or satin stitch.

Place the next pattern piece in position and stitch.

Repeat until all the pieces have been stitched.

Remember to use the same colour thread on the top and in the bobbin of your machine.

The bottom tension of the machine must always be slightly firmer than the top tension so that bits of the bottom stitches are not visible at the top.

First test the length and width of the stitch on a fabric remnant before stitching the pattern pieces. The width of the stitch must be suitable for the design. I normally use a stitch of about 5 or 6 mm (¼ in.) wide. The stitches must be sufficiently dense to prevent the raw edge from showing at the bottom, but not so dense that the stitches lie on top of each other. Stitch in such a way that at least half of the stitching is on the design and the rest on the background fabric.

When stitching a corner, stitch slightly beyond the edge of the fabric. Leaving the needle in the fabric, lift the machine presser foot and turn the article so that you can stitch the other side.

When stitching a V-shape, it is advisable, if your machine allows, to reduce the stitches towards the point of the V. Leave the needle at the point of the V, lift the machine presser foot and turn the article. Lower the presser foot and continue stitching.

If your background fabric tends to bunch while you are sewing zigzag stitches, place thin paper under the article while you stitch. Tear off the paper afterwards.

Hand methods

There are various hand methods for appliqué. I will describe only a few of them.

Paper method

Some needlework stores sell "freezer paper". It is a domestic paper imported from America. It has a shiny layer on one side. The shiny side can be ironed onto the wrong side of fabric. This strengthens the pattern piece so that it is easier to fold the seam allowance over. Remove the paper afterwards by cutting an opening in the backing and pulling it out.

If freezer paper is unobtainable, use ordinary brown paper which is slightly shiny on one side in the same way as described above. First test it to make sure that you will achieve the right results.

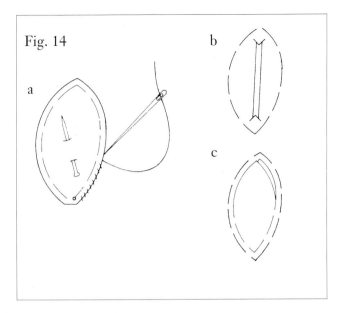

Fig. 14

Trace the design onto the shiny side of the paper and cut it out carefully. Take care to cut out the paper very neatly, since this will determine the ultimate shape of your motif.

Place the shiny side of the paper on the wrong side of the fabric. Take care to place the paper in the right position, particularly when you are using fabric with stripes or prominent designs. Iron the paper onto the fabric.

Cut out the motif, leaving a seam allowance of at least 6 mm (¼ in.). Carefully fold over the seam allowance and tack. Pin the motif to the background fabric and stitch, using tiny stitches (fig. 14a).

If you would rather not tack the seam allowance, pin the motif to the background fabric and fold the seam allowance over to the wrong side with your needle while stitching it with tiny stitches.

Having stitched the motif onto the fabric, remove the paper. Turn the article so that the wrong side faces up. You will see the outlines of the motif clearly because the appliqué stitches are visible. Make a small notch in the background fabric, more or less in the centre of the motif. Insert a small pair of sharp-pointed scissors into the opening and trim all the excess fabric, leaving only 6 mm (¼ in.) of seam allowance next to the appliqué stitches (fig. 14b). Remove the paper. If the motif is long and narrow, such as a leaf, you only need to make the opening in the fabric as it is not necessary to trim the excess fabric at the back (fig. 14c).

Iron-on interfacing method

This method is suitable for motifs that will not be quilted again, since the iron-on interfacing makes it difficult to quilt through all the layers. Iron-on interfacing strengthens an article and prevents loosely woven fabric from pulling.

Place the iron-on interfacing (shiny side up) over the design and peel off each pattern piece. Cut out and iron the interfacing onto the wrong side of the fabric. Add a seam allowance of about 6 mm (¼ in.) around each pattern piece and cut out.

Fold the seam allowance to the wrong side and tack if preferred.

Place the pattern piece onto the background fabric and pin.

If you have not tacked the seam allowance, fold it over as you go.

Now stitch the motif onto the background fabric with small slip-hemming or blind stitches.

Needle-folding method

This is one of the most popular appliqué methods. No iron-on paper or iron-on interfacing is used.

Trace the design onto paper to serve as templates. Cut out the templates. If you are going to use a certain template often, use thin plastic.

Place the templates on the right side of your fabric. Trace the outlines lightly but accurately with a sharp pencil, or use a blue water-soluble pen. Add a seam allowance of about 6 mm (¼ in.) and cut out the pattern pieces from the fabric.

Place a pattern piece on the background fabric with the outlines of the pieces in the right position. Pin (fig. 15).

Use a fairly short thread and a thin, longish, sharp-pointed needle (about no. 10 or 11). Make a knot in the thread. (I always begin folding the fabric on a straight side of a piece, if possible.) Beginning on the wrong side of the background fabric, insert the needle through the background fabric from underneath. Fold the seam allowance of the piece back with your needle (fig. 15b), then insert the needle at the fold of the seam allowance through

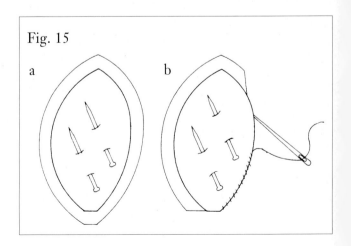

Fig. 15

the fabric of the piece. Insert the needle close to the stitch and down through the background fabric, lift up about 2 mm (⅒ in.) of fabric, and draw the needle through to the top again, through the background fabric and the appliqué motif.

The stitches will be almost invisible on the top layer, but when you turn the article around, the stitches will be clearly visible on the wrong side.

End the stitches on the wrong side of the background fabric.

Motifs with sharp points, such as leaves, must have neat corners. Cut the seam allowance slightly narrower near the point.

Fold in the seam allowance of the first side and stitch up to the point as described above. Trim most of the seam allowance which has also formed a point.

Now fold in the seam allowance of the next side. The seam allowances must not be bulky at the corners; rather trim more of the seam allowance.

Where you have sharp angles, such as at the top of a heart, make a notch in the top of the curve in the corner right up to the outline. Fold the first curve at the top over and stitch up to the notch.

Fold in the seam allowance of the next curve. First make one stitch in the centre at the notch so that it is strengthened there. Insert the needle from underneath through the layers of fabric so that it emerges exactly in the centre of the two curves, about three or four threads from the notch. Sew the stitch straight to the point of the notch. (This stitch is slightly more visible than all the other stitches but will not be too conspicuous if the thread matches the fabric.)

Now begin at the notch and stitch the next curve. Complete the motif.

Blanket stitch appliqué

This technique is particularly suitable for broderie perse appliqué. The motif is stitched to the background with small blanket stitches. This not only strengthens the raw edge of the motif but also looks most attractive.

Use a fabric with pretty designs. Cut a motif from the fabric, adding a small seam allowance of about 6 mm (¼ in.) right around. Place the motif onto the background fabric and pin. (Tack if preferred, but not too close to the edge because the back stitches will be in the way when you stitch the blanket stitches.)

Allow some motifs to overlap for a pleasing overall effect.

Trim sufficient excess fabric from the bottom motif to prevent having to stitch through too many layers of fabric.

Use embroidery or quilting thread for stitching the motifs. Make a knot in the thread and begin on the wrong side of the background fabric. Insert the needle from underneath through all the layers of fabric until it emerges about 6 mm (¼ in.) from the raw edge. Sew small blanket stitches (page 25) right around the motif (fig. 17). The blanket stitches must be spaced close together to prevent the raw edge from showing. End the stitches on the wrong side of the background fabric.

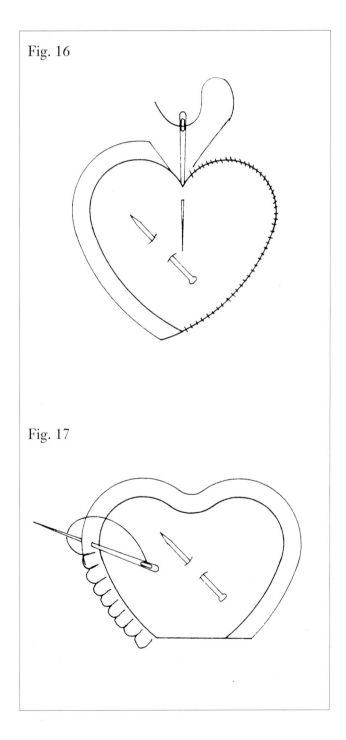

Fig. 16

Fig. 17

Stained-glass or bias binding appliqué

With this technique, the raw edge of the motif which is cut out and placed on the background fabric is covered with bias binding. Then the bias binding is stitched to the background fabric. No seam allowances are added when the pattern pieces are cut out of the fabric.

Paste all the pattern pieces onto the background fabric with a glue stick (Pritt). Tack if you wish, although this is time-consuming. Place the bias binding over the raw edge of each piece. Pin and tack into position. Stitch the bias binding with hemming or blind hemming stitches. Do not allow the edges of the piece to shift out under the bias binding. Where two pieces lie side by side, cover both edges with one strip of bias binding.

Always begin with the piece furthest back on the design.

Both ends of each piece of bias binding must be covered with a next piece of bias binding until the raw edge no longer shows.

Use ready-made bias binding or make it yourself, using either plain or print fabric.

HINT:
You can cut away the background fabric on the seamy side to give appliquéd articles a three-dimensional effect (fig. 14b).

HINT:
To stitch triangles quickly and accurately, you can follow the following method:
● Measure two triangles with seam allowances and determine the size of the square that the triangles will form.
● Split the square exactly in half with a marking pen.
● Mark the stitching lines on both sides of it and stitch.
● Cut the square in half on the cutting line.
● The unfolded triangles form a square.

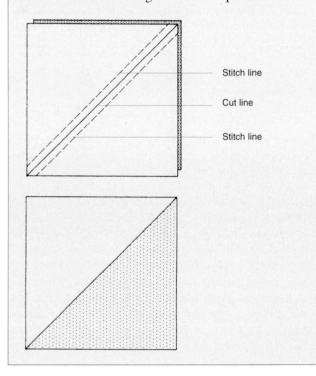

Stitch line

Cut line

Stitch line

22

Stencilling on fabric is very popular. A variety of fabrics may be used, such as cotton, polyester cotton, glazed chintz or linen. It is best to test a piece of fabric before beginning a large project. Rinse the fabric in hot water first to remove all starch and to preshrink it. Textile paint is available from craft shops.

You do not have to use only the patterns in this book for your stencil designs. Copy motifs from your curtains or linen, for example. Use a theme such as shells or, for a nursery, motifs such as teddy bears or trains, and cut your own stencils. Follow the instructions in this book.

Equipment and material for stencilling

Plastic
It is used to cut out stencils.

I like to use the plastic that is used for overhead projectors. It is available from stationery dealers.

Plastic from X-ray films may also be used. Clean old X-ray films with a scouring sponge. This will make them transparent and suitable for stencilling.

Craft knife and cutting board
A sharp-pointed craft knife or scalpel are essential for cutting out stencils. Take care not to damage the working surface with the knife. A cutting board is suitable for this purpose.

Pencil, tracing paper, felt-tip pen
Different kinds of writing material may be used to trace the motif onto the plastic. First test to check whether it can write on the plastic.

Brushes and sponges
Good brushes are needed for neat stencilling. If you are unable to find special stencilling brushes, use a piece of sponge to apply the paint.

Paint
Various kinds of textile paints are obtainable from craft shops and some stationers. The locally manufactured paint is usually much less expensive than the imported kind.

How to stencil
Trace or draw the design on paper. Place the plastic over the design and trace it onto the plastic. The lines must not be easily erased. If the design is too close to the edge of the plastic, you might paint over the edge when you stencil. Cut the pattern from the plastic with your craft knife. Press the design down firmly with your free hand and cut towards you. Rather shift the design than the knife when you come to sharp angles. Make sure that there are always "bridges" in the design. These are narrow strips which are not cut out. If there are not enough bridges, the brush might slip under the stencil, blurring the outlines.

A stencil may also be cut out directly. Place the plastic over the design and use masking tape to secure it. Cut out the stencil directly without tracing any lines on the plastic. The disadvantage of this method is that you will cut up the design at the same time.

Place the stencil on the fabric and secure with masking tape to prevent it from shifting while you work.

Pour a little paint into a small container. Dip the brush into the paint, making sure there is not too much paint on the brush. Press the brush on a piece of paper to prevent smudging. Now paint the openings in the stencil which you want painted. Always paint in the same direction. You could also lightly dab the paint onto the fabric. This will produce a stippled effect.

The paint may also be applied with a sponge. Always make sure there is not too much paint on the sponge.

It is important to remember never to shift the stencil while the paint is still wet. Lift it up carefully. Wipe off any wet paint on the bottom of the stencil before securing it again. Work on a surface that absorbs excess moisture in the paint, such as paper or paper towels.

If you are planning to use more than one colour, it is best to cut out different stencils. For the tablecloth on page 47 I cut two stencils for the strip pattern between the blocks, as well as two for each block. I cut one stencil for the blue dots and yellow leaves, and another one for the green twig and brown circle in the centre of the flower.

When applying more than one colour with the same stencil, the patterns must not be so close together that the different colours overlap should you accidentally paint over the edge of the pattern.

You could even paste masking tape over certain parts before painting the rest. Afterwards you can remove the masking tape and paint the other colour.

If you wish, blend a second colour over the first. With the yellow flowers on the tablecloth, I blended a slightly darker orange with the yellow to produce a shadow effect on the petals.

Embroidery stitches

Since embroidery is employed on some quilts, several embroidery stitches are illustrated (fig. 18).

Blanket stitch

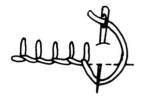

Chain stitch

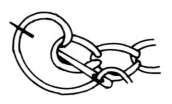

Couching

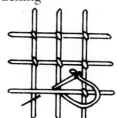

French knot

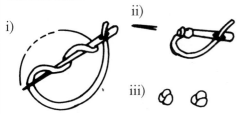

Backstitch

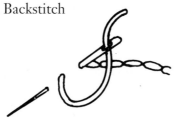

Buttonhole wheel

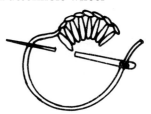

Pekinese (Chinese) stitch

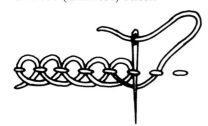

Satin stitch

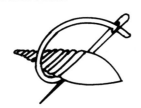

Spider's web

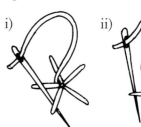

Stem stitch

Feather stitch

Herringbone stitch

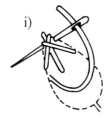

Fly stitch

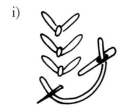

Extended fly stitch

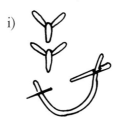
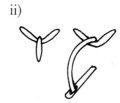

General finishing

Laying out the quilt

The layout of a quilt is an important aspect of quilting. Blocks may be assembled in different ways to produce completely different effects.

Blocks may be joined with sashing between them or butted one against the other. They may be joined either in straight rows or diagonally. One block may be placed in the centre and surrounded by strips with more blocks around the edge.

A few examples are discussed:

Strip layout without sashing (straight-set)

This is one of the simplest methods of joining a quilt. The blocks are joined without sashes around each block, so the patterns flow into each other (an example is the Blackford's Beauty quilt on page 63), or the combined blocks form a pattern (for example the Kaleidoscope quilt on page 41).

Lay the blocks out and decide how you want to arrange them.

Join a row of blocks to form a long strip. Once all the blocks have been joined, the strips are joined (fig. 19).

Strip layout with sashing

Each block is framed by a strip of fabric which accentuates the patterns of the different blocks. The Grandmother's Fan quilt on page 52 is a good example of this method.

Lay the blocks side by side as desired. Cut the strips of fabric for the sashing to the required length. Join the first row of blocks with strips of fabric in between. Repeat the process with all the rows (fig. 22a).

Now cut strips of fabric the same length as the row of blocks. Join the first row of blocks to a strip of fabric (fig. 22b). Stitch the second row of blocks to the other side of the strip of fabric. Add a strip of fabric between each row of blocks in this way until all have been joined. Stitch a strip of fabric onto both the top and bottom of the large patchwork. Stitch a strip of fabric to each side. Now all the blocks will have a frame right around them (fig. 22c).

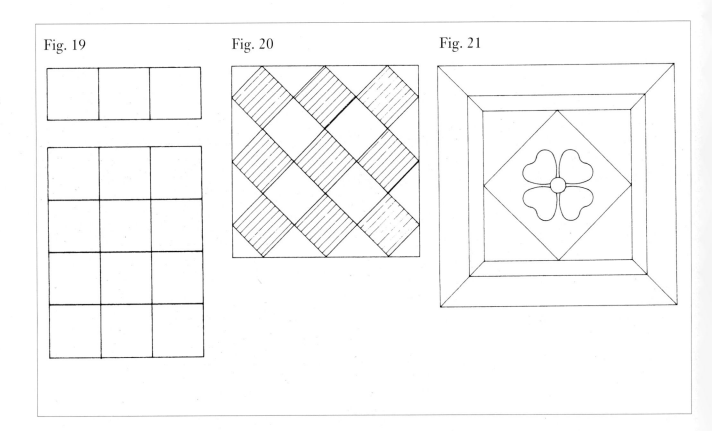

Fig. 19   Fig. 20   Fig. 21

Diagonal layout

With this layout, the blocks are joined diagonally. The blocks appear to slant towards one point, hence the description "on point".

The blocks may be alternated with strips in between, like the Sampler quilt on page 115, or they may be alternated with blocks on which quilting has been applied, such as the Amish quilt on page 71.

Lay the blocks out diagonally. Join halves and quarters to complete. Use the sketch (fig. 20) as an example. First join the blocks in diagonal strips, then join these strips to complete the top layer.

Medallion layout

A block with a particularly striking design may be used as the focal point in a larger article. Place this block horizontally or diagonally. If you position the block horizontally, join four triangles to form a square before adding the next framing strip (fig. 21).

The quilt with the Bushman (San) paintings and proteas on page 116 was joined according to the medallion layout. In this case the block in the centre is much larger than the outer blocks.

The Hearts quilt on page 82 was joined according to another form of medallion layout. The block in the centre forms a focal point with strips joined around it.

Blocks with sashes are subsequently joined right around.

The Cat quilt on page 113 is framed with a strip, after which the different pieced border strips are added.

Adding the borders

Sashes between blocks and border strips around an article influence the effect of the final finishing. You might plan a specific border for your quilt beforehand, but once you have assembled the pieces you might find that it is not suitable. For that reason it is better first to lay out all the blocks once they have been completed, when you will be in a better position to consider the various options for adding the borders.

Keep the following hints in mind:
● The width of the border strips must match the rest of the article.
● The colours used in the borders should match those used in the rest of the quilt. Repeat in the border strip one or more of the colours used in the main quilt.
● Borders must form a unit with the main part of a quilt top. Even if the technique is not the same, it should match the rest of the quilt.

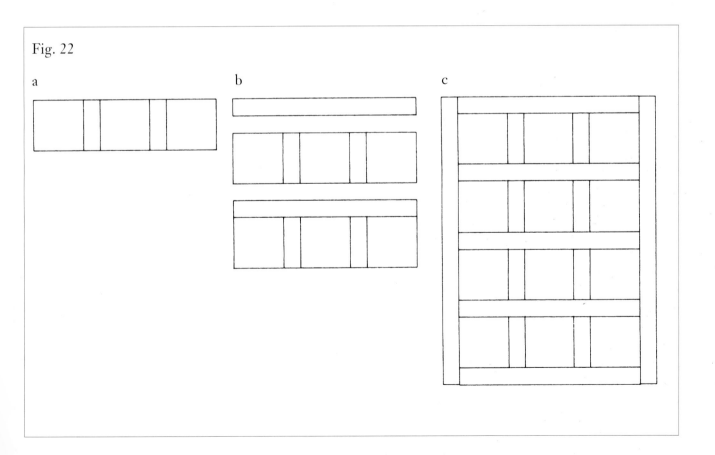

Fig. 22

a

b

c

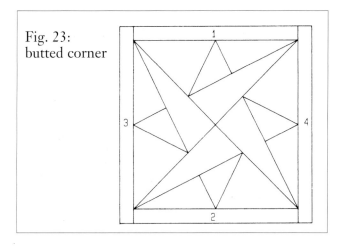

Fig. 23: butted corner

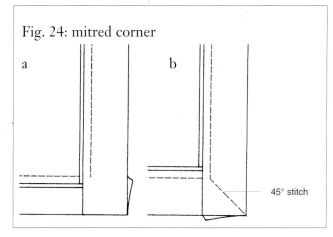

Fig. 24: mitred corner

a   b

45° stitch

Use any of the following techniques for adding a border to a quilt:
● The border may consist of strips of plain or print fabric, such as the black-and-white Log Cabin quilt on page 77.
● Make a border strip as in the Hearts quilt on page 82.
● Appliqué motifs on the border, as in the Broderie perse quilt on page 79.
● Assemble a framing strip from smaller pieces, or use strip piecing as in the Four patch quilt on page 68 and in figure 7 to 10.
● Stencil the border strip, as in the Stencilled table-cloth on page 46.

Joining the border strips

Use the same method for framing smaller articles, such as cushions, and larger articles, such as quilts.

a) With a butted corner (straight borders)

Using a soft pencil, mark four strips as wide as the frame has to be, plus a seam allowance on both sides. Two strips must be as long as the top and bottom of the article and the other two strips as long as the sides plus twice the width of the strips. Cut out the strips.

First stitch the top and bottom strips and then the side strips (fig. 23).

Place the strips on the top layer with right sides facing and raw edges flush. Now stitch and fold over.

If you prefer, you may add corner blocks in the corners of the frame. In this case, cut the border strips as long as the four sides of the article. Cut the corner blocks the same width as the border strips and fill the areas between the border strips.

b) With a mitred corner

Border strips may also be joined at the corners with diagonal or mitred corners. Cut each of the four strips the same length as the article plus twice the width of the strip. For example, if the side of the article is 30 cm long and the border strip is 5 cm (2 in.) wide, the total length of each strip will be 40 cm (16 in.).

Join all the strips to the article, allowing the ends to extend equally at the corners (fig. 24a). Do not stitch into the seam allowance. Lay the article with the stitched border flat, wrong side up. Lift the inner corners of the strips so that the right sides of the strips are together at the corners. Pin the strips together at a 45-degree angle. Stitch, making sure you do not stitch into the seam allowance (fig. 24b). (The fabric of the strips may be folded to one side with a 45-degree angle and flattened with a finger to make a mark along which you can stitch.)

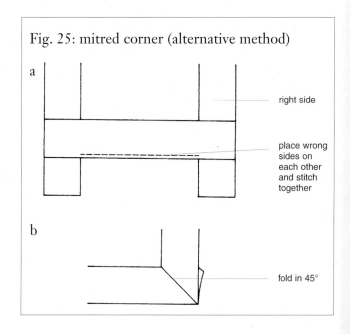

Fig. 25: mitred corner (alternative method)

a

right side

place wrong sides on each other and stitch together

b

fold in 45°

*O*nce the border strips have been stitched to the article, the article is ready for quilting. Quilting consists of stitching through the top layer, the batting and the backing fabric. This may be done by hand, by machine or with flat knots.

If you wish to apply a pattern onto a quilted article, do this before securing the top layer, the batting and the backing with tacking stitches. It will be easier to transfer the pattern accurately.

Trim all excess seam allowances and loose threads, and iron the article neatly.

Mark the quilt patterns on the fabric in one of the following ways:
● Use a water-soluble pen (not the kind that fades after a while). It is usually a blue pen. Rinse the article in clean cold water after quilting and do not iron before the marks have been erased.
● Trace or draw the pattern with a soft pencil if preferred. Special rubbers are available at craft shops for this purpose. Remember, however, not to make unnecessary pencil marks, as these could leave marks.
● Masking tape is suitable for indicating straight lines. Various widths are available – from 6 mm (¼ in.) to about 8 cm (3 in.). The same piece of masking tape may be used more than once. Cut small patterns, for example hearts, from the broader masking tape, paste them onto the fabric and quilt around the tape.
● Dressmaker's carbon paper is also suitable. There must be sufficient contrast between the colour of the paper and that of the fabric for the pattern to show up clearly.
● Use leftover pieces of bath soap or white pencils to produce patterns on darker fabric such as black and navy blue. Draw with the thin edge of the soap.
● White or yellow pencil crayons are also suitable for tracing or drawing patterns on dark fabrics.

To trace a pattern, use a light box or a glass-topped table with a light underneath. Even a windowpane will do for smaller articles. Paste the pattern on the glass with adhesive tape or wonder glue, hold the article over this and trace the pattern with the aid of one of the above. For dark fabrics, proceed as follows: Draw the motif onto paper and cut it out. Trace the pattern onto the fabric, and trace around the pattern.

When the pattern has been transferred onto the article, it is ready for tacking onto the batting and the backing fabric.

Cut the batting and unbleached calico, or any other suitable fabric for the backing, slightly larger than the article you are quilting. (The backing may consist of various fabrics joined until the desired size has been achieved.) Make sure there are no creases in the fabric.

Arrange the layers as follows: backing with the wrong side facing, batting and then the article for quilting, with right side facing (fig. 26). Pin the three layers neatly. Tack firmly with tacking thread of a matching colour, being careful not to crease or fold the fabric. Always begin in the centre and work outwards (fig. 27). A large article such as a bed quilt must be tacked securely to prevent it from shifting or bunching. Tack in straight lines (fig. 28), not

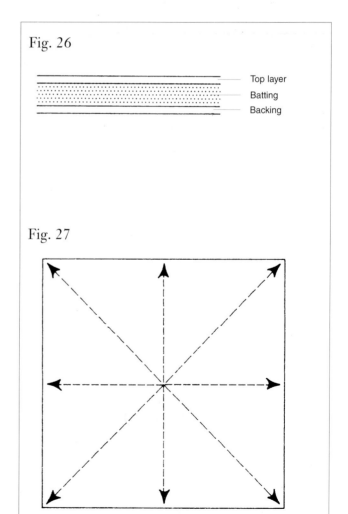

Fig. 26

Top layer
Batting
Backing

Fig. 27

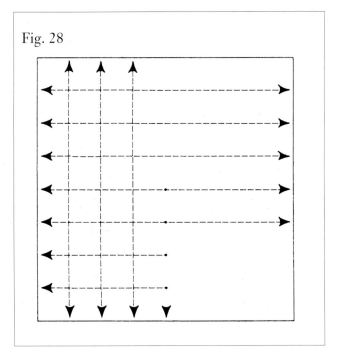

Fig. 28

more than 10 cm (4 in.) apart. The more you tack, the neater the end product.

You may even pin the article with small safety pins. Pin them closely together to prevent the layers from shifting. Take care the thread does not catch on the safety pins while you sew.

A new tool is available that resembles the "gun" used to attach the nylon thread to price tabs on clothing. This may be used to secure the layers. Unfortunately, this tool is not yet readily obtainable. The article is now ready for quilting.

Quilting by hand

Large quilting frames are convenient, especially when several quilters are working on the same project. A disadvantage of a large quilting frame is that it takes up a lot of space and cannot be easily transported. Embroidery frames or quilting hoops are less unwieldy and easier to transport. Some people prefer quilting without a frame.

You will find that thimbles are indispensable when quilting – one for your right middle finger and one for the index finger of your left hand, especially when tackling a large article with a great deal of quilting. Practise until you are able to quilt wearing thimbles, as this will save you much inconvenience. Your quilting thread should be about 45 cm (18 in.) long. Use a special quilting needle.

Make a holding knot at one end of the thread. Begin in the centre of the article and work to the

outside. Insert the needle from underneath through the fabric about 2 cm (¾ in.) from the point where you want to begin, and draw the thread through at the point where you want to begin quilting. (Some people prefer beginning from the top.) Pull the knot through the backing, leaving it in the batting (fig. 29a and b). Continue tacking with small running (basting) stitches through all three layers.

The size of the stitches is up to you: you may even work as finely as ten stitches per 2 cm (¾ in.). The stitches must be regular and even and must be clearly visible on the other side. Insert the needle through all the layers from the top. Hold one hand underneath the fabric and feel with your index finger (the one with the thimble) whether the needle has penetrated through all the layers of fabric, then draw the needle through to the top again. Sew three or four small stitches at a time before pulling the thread tight. Take care not to pull the thread too tight, because this will result in small pleats forming.

Initially you will probably sew only one or two stitches at a time, but with practice you will be able to sew three or four stitches at a time before pulling the thread through. Continue tacking until the thread is about 10 cm (4 in.) long.

To finish, insert the needle from underneath into the fabric. Make a knot in the thread close to the fabric before stitching the last stitch. Sew one more stitch through the fabric and the batting so that the knot is caught in the batting. (Some people end with a backstitch, but it should not be visible.) Pull the thread through to the backing and cut off against the fabric.

If you are using a round quilting frame, it is advisable to use more than one threaded needle at the

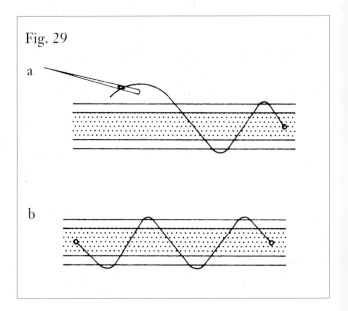

Fig. 29

a

b

same time. Begin with each needle inside the quilting frame and quilt your lines or patterns until you reach the edge of the frame, but do not finish off the thread. Move the frame so that the needles are at the beginning of the frame again. This will save time and you will not need to adjust the frame after each small piece of quilting.

Machine quilting

Machine quilting is gaining popularity in our hurried lives today. Virtually any motif may be machine quilted. It is much faster than hand quilting.

Various motifs, such as feathers, hearts, animals and leaves, as well as straight lines running parallel, crossing each other to form a square, or stitched diagonally to form a checkered pattern may be machine quilted.

Use the same nylon or ordinary thread you would use for dressmaking and other sewing projects. Certain kinds of nylon threads tend to be hard and may damage the fabric, so select your nylon thread carefully.

As for quilting by hand, iron the article first. Mark the stitching lines with a water-soluble pen on the top layer before pinning or basting it firmly to the batting.

If you secure the layers with pins instead of basting stitches, you will not need to waste time unpicking the tacking stitches.

Use a special presser foot, also called the "walking foot", for your machine when you quilt large articles. An ordinary presser foot is suitable for smaller articles. The "walking foot" makes it easier to feed the fabric through more smoothly and neatly since it secures the fabric from the top, feeding it back through the feeding mechanism of the machine. The fabric layers will be less inclined to shift.

Machine quilting may also be done while the feeding mechanism of the machine is lowered. This is particularly suitable for quilting motifs. Use your machine's presser foot and push the article evenly through with your hand while running the machine. Roll up the article tightly but carefully so that it fits under the machine. Begin quilting in the centre of the article while following the pattern marks you made.

It is best first to transfer the motifs you want to quilt on a remnant of fabric and to practise in order to quilt evenly.

The Fish quilt on page 53 was machine quilted in flowing random movements, which is particularly suitable for this quilt because it creates an impression of moving water.

Different quilting techniques
There are various quilting techniques but we will discuss only a few of these.

Design quilting
Design quilting looks striking on open areas. You may even use specific designs, such as leaves, animals, hearts, feathers and flowers. Enlarge or reduce the pattern with a photocopier to fit neatly into the area where you want to quilt. The flowers in the Grandmother's Fan quilt on page 52 and the Broderie perse quilt on page 79 are examples of this technique.

Border quilting
Border quilting frames an article and usually consists of flowing, repetitive patterns. The chain pattern on the border strips of the Grandmother's Fan quilt on page 52 is an example. The pattern may be adjusted to make it fit onto the strip of fabric. Sew a few shorter or longer stitches to make the pattern fit into the space.

Outline quilting
This is one of the most popular quilting techniques. Stitch 4 mm (⅛ in.) to 8 mm (¼ in.) away from the seam edge of a pattern piece, as in the Windmill quilt on page 55. If preferred, no additional marking is necessary, since the seam line is followed.

Blind or stitch-in-the-ditch quilting
Here the quilting is done in the seam line between two pieces. It may also be applied close to the seam line on the side where the seam allowance has been folded over so that you do not have to stitch through all the layers of fabric. This produces a puffed effect and will make your pattern appear more prominent. I used blind quilting around the Table Mountain motif on the Table Mountain wall hanging on page 111.

Echo or contour quilting
This quilting forms contour lines around the motif. It consists of regular lines that follow the shape of the motif until all the space has been filled up. With smaller articles the lines are between 6 mm (¼ in.) and 1 cm (½ in.) apart, but with larger articles such as bed quilts the lines may be further apart.

Background quilting
A poorly quilted article tends to form lumps after washing. For this reason background quilting is used on large open spaces. Straight or curved lines, or a combination of the two, are equally effective. Background quilting with straight lines was used for the Broderie perse quilts on pages 72 and 79.

Tying with thread
A flat knot may be used to hold the three layers together so that no quilting stitches are visible. Insert the needle through all the layers of fabric from the right side, leaving the end of the thread about 10 cm (4 in.) long. Sew a backstitch and leave another piece of thread at the other end. Make a double knot and cut the thread 2,5 cm (1 in.) from the fabric. The threads form part of the decoration. A Trip around the World quilt looks very attractive if all the flat knots are worked through the fabric. The knots may be made in the centre of each block, or at the corners where the blocks meet.

Quilting thread, perle cotton, embroidery thread or fine crochet thread are used for this purpose.

Finishing the edges of articles

There are various methods for finishing the edges of articles such as wall hangings and quilts. I will describe some of the most popular bindings.

Double binding
Cut out the fabric for the binding to the required length. For example, if you want an edge of 2 cm (1 in.), it must be 4 cm (2 in.) wide (for the front and back), multiplied by two (because the fabric is folded in half). Add seam allowances of 6 mm. You must therefore cut out 9,2 cm (4½ in.) wide strips of fabric. The length of the strips is as long as the sides of the article plus the width of the strips.

Fold the strip of fabric in half with wrong sides facing and raw edges together. Place the raw edges of the strip (binding) against the raw edges of the article on the right side and stitch along the seam line (fig. 30a and b). Make mitred corners in the binding at the corners of the article. Fold the binding corner over and cut off the excess fabric at the corner.

Fold another mitred corner at the back of the binding and stitch. Fold the remaining binding over until it is 2 cm (1 in.) wide and stitch to the back along the stitching line, using small stitches.

Folded-over mitred corner
To shape the corners neatly, fold the seam allowance diagonally across the corner of the article. Cut the end off (fig. 31a) and fold both sides towards each other to form a mitred corner (45-degree angle) (fig. 31b). Stitch the two folded edges with fine stitches (fig. 31c).

Inverted or bound edge
For an article with curved corners, bias binding is used at the corners, although straight strips are also suitable.

Cut out the top layer, the batting and the backing

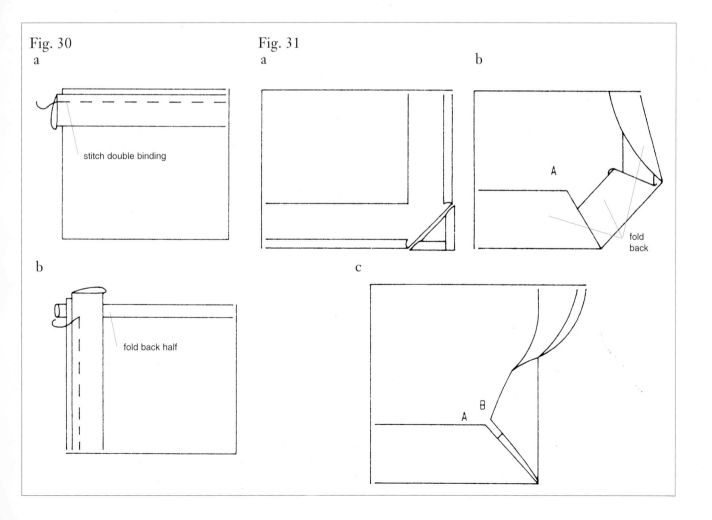

Fig. 30

a

stitch double binding

b

fold back half

Fig. 31

a

b

A

fold
back

c

B

A

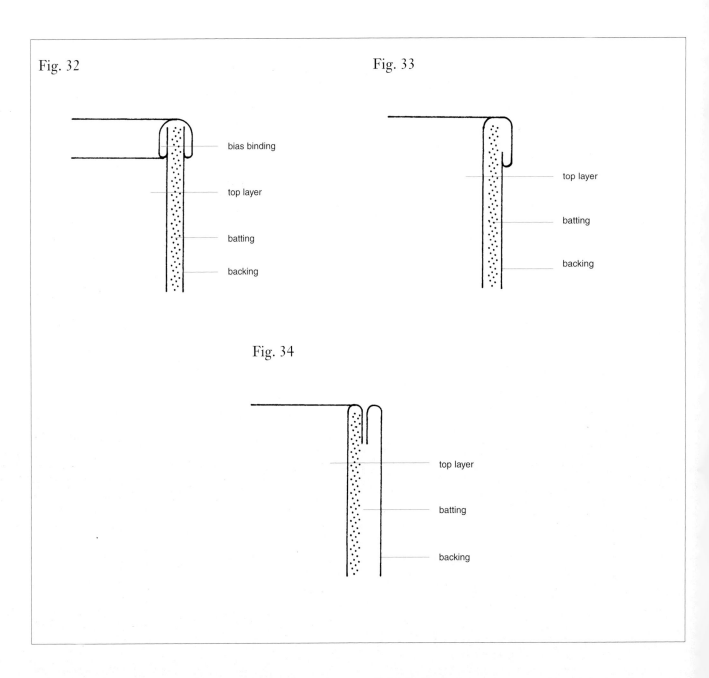

Fig. 32

bias binding

top layer

batting

backing

Fig. 33

top layer

batting

backing

Fig. 34

top layer

batting

backing

(unbleached calico) neatly. Cut the strips to the desired length. Place together a strip and the article right sides facing and stitch 1 cm (¼ in.) from the side of the article through all the layers. (Adjust the seam allowance if necessary.) Fold the raw edges of the binding over about 1 cm (¼ in.). Secure with hemming stitches. Always take care the first machine stitching is not visible (fig. 32).

Folded-over edge (to the back)
A folded-over edge is useful when you do not want a prominent additional binding for the edges.

Cut the edges of the article 3 cm (1¼ in.) to 4 cm (1½ in.) larger than the batting and the backing. Fold the edge over as for a hem and stitch with hemming stitches (fig. 33).

Folded-closed edge
Cut the top and bottom the same size and the batting about 1 cm (¼ in.) smaller. Fold the edges of the top and bottom pieces between the layers and secure with small stitches (fig. 34).

NOTE:
It is important to fill the edges with batting as well. When you trim the additional batting you must make provision for this so that sufficient batting remains to fill the edge.

General information

● Seam allowances have not been added to the templates at the back of the book.

● Where any other parts, for example strips of fabric for borders, have to be cut out, seam allowances have been added unless indicated otherwise. The seam allowance is 6 mm (¼ in.) throughout unless indicated otherwise.

● The quantity of fabric required is calculated according to fabric measuring 1,15 m (45 in.) wide unless indicated otherwise. Adjust the quantities for wider or narrower fabric.

● The quantity of batting is calculated according to batting measuring 1,5 m (60 in.).

● Where smaller articles are made from remnants it is difficult to indicate quantities with the list of materials. Use the photograph and/or pattern as a guide, as well as the completed size indicated for wall hangings and miniature quilts.

HINTS:
● Cut out the longest strips from the fabric first.

● When cutting strips of fabric for borders, etc. it is advisable first to measure whether the strips have to be the same length as the measurements in the pattern. The strips may have to be slightly longer if you have not worked a hundred per cent accurately. When you trace the templates it is often a fraction of a millimetre on both sides. The tip of the pencil or pen is responsible for this. Keep this in mind when you cut border strips.

● In some cases I supplied only the width of the border strip and not the length, since you can do the measurements once your pattern has been completed.

● The quantity of batting and backing is always a little more than required. Before folding over the binding, trim any excess batting and backing. Make sure you have sufficient batting left over to fill the binding up to the point where it is folded over.

● Join pieces of batting if it is too narrow for a large quilt. Place the two pieces of batting together. Secure with large, loose oversewing (topsewing) stitches, but take care a thick ridge is not formed.

● If the fabric is too small for the backing, join different pieces to obtain the right size. Remnants from the top layer may be used for this purpose to make the backing more interesting.

● Sometimes the quantity of materials is more than required. Use the remnants to make small articles such as cushions or join it for the reverse side of a project.

● When two pieces with curves or sharp angles are stitched together, make notches in the seam allowance before you turn the right side out.

● Cut off any excess seam allowance before you turn the right side out.

● Use patchwork patterns and stencil motifs for quilt patterns.

American Jewels quilt

This quilt was made from fabric remnants. The blocks consist of four squares which are joined, as well as two rectangles which are also joined. In turn, these are joined to form patterns.

The background is a light-coloured fabric, while the darker fabric forms the pattern. The quilt is joined with the machine and is therefore a quick way of using up fabric remnants.

TECHNIQUES: machine or hand piecing; hand quilting; general

	Wall quilt	**Single**	**Double**	**King-size**
Size when completed	1,15 m x 1,15 m (45 in. x 45 in.)	1,35 m x 2,15 m (53 in. x 86 in.)	2,15 m x 2,15 m (86 in. x 86 in.)	2,55 m x 2,15 m (102 in. x 86 in.)
Number of blocks with squares	32	88	160	196
Number of squares with triangles	32	92	164	200
Size of blocks 10 cm (4 in.) x 10 cm (4 in.)				
Materials				
variety of dark-coloured fabric remnants	1,5 m (1¾ yd)	2,8 m (3 yds)	3,5 m (4 yds)	4 m (4¾ yds)
light-coloured fabric for background	1,5 m (1¾ yd)	2,8 m (3 yds)	3,5 m (4 yds)	4 m (4¾ yds)
fabric for border strip, 4 cm (1½ in.) wide (burgundy)	40 cm (½ yd)	50 cm (½ yd)	70 cm (¾ yd)	80 cm (⅞ yd)
fabric for border strip, 11 cm (4½ in.) wide (dark-blue)	70 cm (¾ yd)	1 m (1¾ yd)	1,4 m (1½ yd)	1,6 m (1⅞ yd)
fabric for edge binding, 5 cm (2 in.) wide (burgundy)	40 cm (½ yd)	70 cm (1¾ yd)	90 cm (1 yd)	1 m (1⅓ yd)
fabric for backing	1,5 m (1¾ yd)	2,8 m (3¼ yds)	5 m (6 yds)	6 m (7 yds)
batting	1 m (1⅓ yd)	2,2 m (2½ yds)	4 m (4¾ yds)	4,5 m (5 yds)
pattern (page 118)				

Use a light-coloured fabric for the background. Use either a variety of fabric remnants in light colours, or the same fabric throughout.

The fabric forming the patterns must be dark to achieve a bold contrast between the background and the patterns.

Half of the blocks in the quilt have squares, of which two must be in light and two in dark colours. The other half of the blocks have two triangles, of which one triangle is made up with light colours and the other triangle of dark colours. These blocks are joined in fours to make a larger square which ultimately forms the pattern. This quilt is easy to make and may be joined either by hand or with a machine.

- Cut out the templates from the fabric.
- Join the small squares (template 1[i]) in pairs with right sides facing so that one piece is light and the other dark.
- Join these strips in pairs with right sides facing. These form squares.
- Join two of the squares to form a triangle. Join two more squares. Join the two rectangles to form a square.
- Make sure that four dark blocks meet in the centre to form a dark square.
- Join the triangles (template 1 [ii]) so that one light triangle and one dark triangle combined form a square (page 118).
- Join the squares in pairs to the dark triangles side by side to form a rectangle. Join two of the rectan-

gles, so that the dark triangles form a large square in the centre. Use the photograph as a guide.

● Join the blocks with the triangles and the squares alternately, thus completing the centre part of the quilt.

● Cut out a 5,2 cm (2 in.) wide strip of fabric for the burgundy border strip and join around the centre part.

● Make the pieced border strip by joining templates A, B and C. (Use strip piecing [page 16] if preferred.) Join this strip around the burgundy border strip.

● Cut out a 12,2 cm (5 in.) strip of fabric for the dark-blue border strip and join.

● Place the top layer with right sides facing on the batting and the backing. Tack securely.

● Quilt the article. Use outline quilting if you wish.

● Cut a 6,2 cm (2½ in.) strip from the burgundy fabric for the framing. Place with right sides together against the raw edge of the quilt and stitch through all the layers.

● Fold in a 6 mm (¼ in.) hem and fold half of the fabric over. Stitch to the back with small hemming stitches.

TECHNIQUES: folded-over method; general

MATERIALS
simple, bought jacket pattern
black velvet, satin and different gold-coloured
  fabrics (according to the pattern)
lining fabric (according to the pattern)

Use a simple, bought pattern for making the jacket.

● Cut out the pattern from the backing fabric.
● Cut strips varying from 2 cm (1 in.) to 4 cm (2 in.)
out of the different fabrics. If you wish, make all the
strips the same width.
● Decide which strips should be partly black and

partly gold. First join these strips before stitching
them to the backing.
● The entire jacket is made according to the folded-
over method. Begin at one side of each piece and
work towards the other side.
● Place the first strip with right side facing on the
backing.
● Place the next strip with right side facing on the
first strip and stitch.
● Fold the strip with right side facing up. Pin and
place the next strip on top with right side facing.
● Proceed until the entire piece is covered.
● Complete all the pieces in this way.
● Now stitch the pieces according to the instructions in your pattern.

Kaleidoscope quilt and Shell wall hanging

The Kaleidoscope quilt (page 42) is beautiful on the antique iron-and-brass bed. The Shell wall hanging (page 42) is a perfect match with the quilt and complements the room with its combination of antique and modern accessories. The Kaleidoscope quilt is joined with the paper-pieced method and quilted by hand with fine stitches.

The inlay method is used for the Shell wall hanging and is richly embellished with beads and sequins of different sizes and shapes.

Note the good use of colour in the quilt and the wall hanging.

Kaleidoscope quilt

TECHNIQUES: paper-based machine patchwork; hand quilting; general

The kaleidoscope pattern is a traditional pattern which may be arranged in many different shapes to look different each time. The three different templates each appear four times in the 15 cm (6 in.) x 15 cm (6 in.) square.

Colour value also plays an important role in this quilt, in other words depending on whether the fabric is a light, medium or dark colour. It could even be medium light or medium dark. (Read more about the colour value of fabric on page 11.)

Make photocopies of the pattern chart in this book. You could even make photocopies of the close-up photograph of the quilt. Examine the colours in your fabrics. Divide according to a colour and a colour value. Decide which colours you wish to use, and where, then colour in the pattern accordingly.

To make a block, proceed as follows:
● Join piece C to piece B and piece A to the other side of piece B.
● Join piece C to piece B and piece A to the other side of piece B. Join the two quarters to form half a square (fig. 12).
● Repeat the process to complete the other half of the square and stitch the two halves.
● If you wish to follow the paper-based machine method on page 18, first complete one half and then the other half. In this way you will not have to work in quarters.
● Complete all the blocks.
● Join the blocks in rows.
● Join the rows.
● Place the joined quilt top with right side facing over the batting and the backing. Tack securely.
● Quilt by hand through all three layers.
● Fold over a hem in the raw edges of the quilt top. Stitch to the back with small hemming stitches.

	Wall quilt	Single	Double	King-size
Size when completed	90 cm x 1,05 m (36 in. x 42 in.)	1,3 m x 2,1 m (52 in. x 86 in.)	2,1 m x 2,25 m (86 in. x 90 in.)	2,25 m x 2,25 m (90 in x 90 in.)
Layout of blocks	6 x 7	10 x 14	14 x 15	17 x 15
Total number of blocks	42	140	210	225
Materials				
variety of fabric remnants	1,5 m (1¾ yd)	4 m (4¾ yds)	6,5 m (7½ yds)	8 m (9 yds)
fabric for the 5 cm (2 in.) wide border strip (if preferred)	35 cm (½ yd)	50 cm (½ yd)	65 cm (¾ yd)	1 m (1⅓ yd)
fabric for backing	1,3 m (1½ yd)	3 m (3½ yds)	4 m (4½ yds)	5,2 m (6 yds)
batting	1,3 m (1½ yd)	1,8 m (2 yds)	5 m (6 yds)	5,5 m (6¼ yds)
bias binding for framing patterns (page 119)				

Shell wall hanging

TECHNIQUES: inlay method; machine piecing; hand quilting; embroidery; folded-star method; general

Completed size is about 1,3 m (52 in.) x 1 m (40 in.)

MATERIALS
variety of fabric remnants
1,35 m (1¾ yd) fabric for backing
1,35 m (1¾ yd) batting
sequins
beads
variety of thread

Because of insufficient space the pattern for the wall hanging is not supplied, but only instructions for making it.

● Use the photograph as a guide and draw the two shells on a large piece of paper. Notice how the shells have been subdivided into smaller pieces and the use of colour in the fabrics.
● Trace exactly the same pattern on another piece of paper. Number the pattern parts so that they correspond on both papers.
● Colour both patterns in the same colour according to the fabric you have. One pattern will be cut up for templates, while the other pattern will be kept intact to allow you to join the templates accordingly.
● Follow the instructions for the inlay method on page 14 and stitch the pattern pieces together.
● The background consists of squares which are laid out in an irregular pattern. They may be joined by machine or by hand. (Follow one of the methods discussed earlier on page 12 or 13.)
● Appliqué the shells onto the background.
● Decorate the wall hanging with sequins and beads for a three-dimensional effect. Embroidery stitches may also be employed.
● Join strips of fabric to form a border strip and stitch.
● Place the top layer on the batting and the backing. Quilt through all the layers.
● Fold the fabric of the border strip back, fold in a small hem and stitch with hemming stitches.
● Decorate the top layer further with star points (page 13) which are joined to form strips.

TECHNIQUES: strip piecing; hand quilting; general

	Wall quilt	Single	Double	King-size
Size when completed	1,5 m x 1,5 m	1,5 m x 2 m	2 m x 2 m	2,4 m x 2,4 m
	(60 in. x 60 in.)	(60 in. x 80 in.)	(80 in. x 80 in.)	(94 in. x 94 in.)
Size of stars in m	1,23 (50 in.)	1,23 (50 in.)	1,44 (57 in.)	1,54 (60 in.)
Border strips	12 cm (4¾ in.)	12 cm (4¾ in.)	26 cm (10¼ in.)	40 cm (15¾ in.)
Additional strips: top and bottom	–	15 cm	–	–
Materials				
colour 1: dark blue	8 cm (⅛ yd)	8 cm (⅛ yd)	20 cm (¼ yd)	30 cm (⅜ yd)
colour 2: white with blue	15 cm (¼ yd)	15 cm (¼ yd)	30 cm (⅜ yd)	35 cm (½ yd)
colour 3: black with white	25 cm (⅜ yd)	25 cm (⅜ yd)	40 cm (½ yd)	50 cm (⅝ yd)
colour 4: maroon	30 cm (⅜ yd)	30 cm (⅜ yd)	50 cm (⅝ yd)	55 cm (⅝ yd)
colour 5: wine red with white	50 cm (⅝ yd)	50 cm (⅝ yd)	80 cm (⅞ yd)	90 cm (1 yd)
colour 6: dark-blue print	30 cm (⅜ yd)	30 cm (⅜ yd)	50 cm (⅝ yd)	55 cm (⅝ yd)
colour 7: light-blue print	30 cm (⅜ yd)	30 cm (⅜ yd)	50 cm (5⅝ yds)	55 cm (⅝ yd)
colour 8: white with maroon	25 cm (⅜ yd)	25 cm (⅜ yd)	40 cm (½ yd)	50 cm (⅝ yd)
background fabric	1 m (1⅛ yd)	1,5 m (1¾ yd)	2 m (2¼ yds)	2,5 m (3 yds)
border strip fabric	1 m (1⅛ yd)	1,2 m (1⅜ yd)	2,4 m (2¾ yds)	4 m (4½ yds)
framing fabric	50 cm (⅝ yd)	70 cm (¾ yd)	80 cm (⅞ yd)	90 cm (1 yd)
backing fabric	1,5 m x 1,5 m	1,5 m x 2 m	2 m x 2 m	2,5 m x 2,5 m
	(1¾ yd x 1¾ yd)	(1¾ yd x 2¼ yds)	(2¼ yds x 2¼ yds)	(2¾ yds x 2¾ yds)
batting	1,5 m x 1,5 m	1,5 m x 2 m	2 m x 2 m	2,5 m x 2,5 m
	(1¾ yd x 1¾ yd)	(1¾ yd x 2¼ yds)	(2¼ yds x 2¼ yds)	(2¾ yds x 2¾ yds)

● Use a long ruler and rotary cutter and cut out 6 cm (2½ in.) wide strips plus 6 mm (¼ in.) seam allowance on both sides, thus 7,2 cm (3 in.) wide, for the wall quilt and single-bed quilt.
● Use a long ruler and rotary cutter and cut out 7 cm-strips (2¾ in.) plus a 6 mm (¼ in.) seam allowance on both sides, thus 8,2 cm (3¼ in.) wide, for the double-bed quilt.
● Use a long ruler and rotary cutter and cut out 7,5 cm (3 in.) strips plus a 6 mm (¼ in.) seam allowance on both sides, thus 8,7 cm (3½ in.), for the king-size bed quilt.
● Join the strips. The following combination for assembling the strips was used for the quilt on the photograph:
1-2-3-4-5-6
2-3-4-5-6-7
3-4-5-6-7-8
4-5-6-7-8-9
5-6-7-8-9-10
6-7-8-9-10-11
● Use a protractor or a ruler with the 45-degree line. Subdivide the strips to form diamonds (fig. 35a). Make sure the angle is exactly 45 degrees. It may be necessary to adjust the angle after having cut three or four times to obtain an accurate 45-degree angle again because of the movement of the fabric.
● Join the strips to form a diamond (fig. 35b).

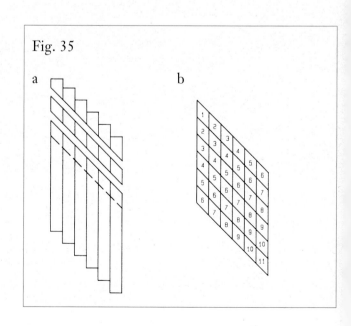

Fig. 35
a   b

● Join eight diamonds to form a star. When the diamonds are joined a Y-seam is stitched. This means that you do not stitch in the seam allowance where the two parts meet in the fork of the Y. Press the seam allowances open. This will make it easier to join the background triangles and squares. (This is one of the few occasions when a seam allowance is opened up in patchwork.)

● When you cut out the triangles and squares for the background it is advisable to cut them slightly larger than necessary.

● Join the triangles and squares. Trim any excess seam allowance.

● Join the border strips as preferred.

● Tack the quilt top to the batting and the backing. Quilt the article.

● Use one of the methods on page 34 to 35 for the binding.

Stencilled tablecloth

TECHNIQUES: stencilling; machine patchwork; quilting; general

The yellow-and-blue stencilled tablecloth has a fresh look. You can paint a plain-coloured cloth to match your colour scheme and interior decorating. The tablecloth has different blocks and strips of material which are painted and then joined.

Increase the number of blocks and repeat the patterns to make a bed quilt.

	Table cloth	Single	Double	King-size
Size when completed	1 m x 1,1 m (40 in. x 44 in.)	1,5 m x 2,02 m (60 in. x 81 in.)	2,02 m x 2,02 m (81 in. x 81 in.)	2,54 m x 2,54 m (102 in. x 102 in.)
Layout of blocks	2 x 2	3 x 4	4 x 4	5 x 5
Total number of blocks	4	12	16	25
Size of blocks 30 cm (12 in.) x 30 cm (12 in.)				
Strips of 30 cm x 22 cm (12 in. x 9 in.)	4	17	24	40
Inlay blocks of 22 cm x 22 cm (9 in. x 9 in.)	1	6	9	16
Materials				
fabric for top layer	1,8 m (2 yds)	4,5 m (5 yds)	6 m (6¾ yds)	7 m (7¾ yds)
fabric for backing	1,5 m (1¾ yd)	3 m (3½ yds)	5 m (5½ yds)	6 m (6¾ yds)
batting	1,2 m (1⅜ yd)	2,5 m (2¾ yds)	4 m (4½ yds)	5 m (5½ yds)
textile paint according to colour choice 10 cm (4 in.) wide border strip pattern (pages 120, 121 and 122)				

● Cut the number of blocks and strips from the top layer fabric according to the sizes and numbers indicated, and add seam allowances.
● Follow the instructions on page 23 for stencilling.
● Iron the fabric neatly.
● Join the blocks and strips (page 26).
● Place the top layer on the batting and the backing and tack to secure.
● Outline quilt the motifs.
● Quilt the border patterns.
● Trim excess batting and backing.

● Fold over the raw edges of the front, fold in a hem and stitch with small hemming stitches.

HINT:
You can even paint the tablecloth on one big piece of material without dividing it into strips and blocks.

TECHNIQUES: machine piecing; hand piecing; embroidery; general

	Wall quilt	Single	Double	King-size
Size when completed	1,1 m x 1,1 m	1,4 m x 2 m	2,1 m x 2,1 m	2,5 m x 2,5 m
	(44 in. x 44 in.)	(56 in. x 80 in.)	(84 in. x 84 in.)	(100 in. x 100 in.)
Materials				
variety of fabric remnants	2,5 m (2¾ yds)	5 m (6 yds)	7 m (8 yds)	8 m (9 yds)
fabric for backing	1,2 m (13/8 yds)	3 m (3½ yds)	5 m (5¾ yds)	6 m (6¾ yds)
batting (if preferred)	1,1 m (1¼ yd)	2 m (2¼ yds)	4,2 m (5 yds)	5 m (5¾ yds)

The choice of fabric is important in crazy quilting. Fabrics must have the right texture. Velvet, corduroy, tweed, thick bridal satin, dralon, etc. are popular choices.

A crazy quilt usually resembles an antique quilt. It may also hold many memories. A variety of materials and objects are used to embellish it, the most common being embroidery stitches in various kinds of wool and thread. Old pieces of lace, small crochet doilies, buttons and other small charms, school badges and university or other badges may also serve as decoration. Even photographs can be transferred to a quilt.

The following interesting elements were embroidered on this quilt: names or initials of family members, the name of the family farm, bunches of grapes, names of pets, dates of weddings, and dates of births and deaths of previous generations.

● Collect all the fabric remnants you intend using. Decide whether you first want to join some parts, to be used later with smaller pieces, for example a fan. (Use the photograph as a guide.)
● Cut out and join the pieces of fabric as you go. (You can sew the pieces onto a foundation fabric, although then it is very thick.) The fabric pieces do not have to have any particular shape.
● The raw edges of the fabric do not always have to be folded in, especially if the fabric is very thick and will not fray. Use embroidery stitches to stitch the seam lines. This will serve both as decoration and to strengthen the article.
● Take care to spread the different fabrics equally over the quilt, so that a certain fabric does not appear in only one part of the quilt.
● Join the fabric pieces until the desired size is achieved.
● Decorate with embroidery stitches as preferred.
● Sew buttons and other objects onto the quilt.
● Place the top layer on the batting (if used) and the backing, and make a folding edge (page 34). (You may prefer a binding around the quilt as described on page 33, or you may want to place the backing and top layer together, right sides facing, and stitch all round the outer edge. Leave a sufficiently large opening and turn right side out. Stitch the opening.)
● Rather than quilting, use flat knots to hold the layers neatly together (page 32). Decide what you prefer. Traditionally, quilts were usually simply tied with flat knots without batting. When batting was used, it was a lightweight kind.

Log Cabin quilt for a nursery

This is a modern version of a Log Cabin quilt. The square in the centre of each block consists of fabric with motifs. The theme of the motifs is the universe. It begins with squares with the sun, moon, stars and planets on them. Other squares have faces of people drawn on them. Further down there are squares with various animals. It is a really lovely quilt for children.

The quilt is made according to the folded-over method, but the strips have different widths. The strips are cut at an angle and virtually all have different widths. This is an ideal way of using up fabric remnants.

TECHNIQUES: folded-over method; machine piecing; machine quilting; general

	Wall quilt	Single	Double	King-size
Size when completed	80 cm x 80 cm	1,4 m x 2,5 m	2 m x 2,5 m	2,5 m x 2,5 m
	(32 in. x 32 in.)	(56 in. x 99 in.)	(79 in. x 99 in.)	(99 in. x 99 in.)
Layout of blocks	3 x 3	4 x 9	7 x 9	9 x 9
Total number of blocks	9	36	63	81
Size of blocks 21 cm (8¼ in.) x 21 cm (8¼ in.)				
Materials				
plain fabric remnants (for framing around squares)	2 m (2¼ yds)	5 m (5½ yds)	8 m (9 yds)	10 m (11¼ yds)
fabric remnants with motives for the centre square of the blocks	40 cm (½ yd)	1,6 m (2 yds)	2,4 m (2¾ yds)	3,2m (3⅝ yds)
fabric for the blue 4,7 cm (1⅞ in.) wide border	40 cm (½ yd)	50 cm (⅝ yd)	70 cm (¾ yd)	1 m (1⅓ yd)
print fabric for the broad border strip	1 m (1⅓ yd)	2,2 m (2½ yds)	2,5 m (2⅞ yds)	3 m (3½ yds)
fabric for framing	40 cm (½ yd)	50 cm (½ yd)	70 cm (¾ yd)	1 m (1⅓ yd)
fabric for backing	1 m (1⅓ yd)	3 m (3½ yds)	5,2 m (6 yds)	7 m (8 yds)
batting	1 m (1⅓ yd)	2,7 m (3 yds)	4 m (4¾ yds)	5 m (5½ yds)

● Cut out a square from a pretty fabric with a motif for the square in the centre of the block. For this quilt the squares were about 13 cm (5¼ in.) x 13 cm (5¼ in.).
● Cut strips from the plain fabric. All the strips in the quilt are cut at a slight angle for a more interesting effect.
● Join the strips around the square using the folded-over method described on page 15.
● Once all the blocks have been completed, finish them to measure 22,2 cm (8⅞ in.) x 22,2 cm (8⅞ in.).
● Join the blocks.
● Cut out the blue border strip and join all around the pieced blocks.
● Cut out another broad border strip and join all around as well. The border strip may consist of several fabrics joined together to achieve the desired length.
● The border strip of the quilt on the photograph is 25 cm wide. Change the width if preferred.
● Place the top layer right side up on the batting and the backing. Tack.
● Machine quilt the quilt. Either use outline quilting around the blocks, or quilt random patterns on it.
● Cut out a 5 cm (2 in.) wide strip of fabric for the framing.
● Place with right sides together against the raw edge of the quilt and stitch through all the layers.
● Fold in a 1 cm hem, then fold half the fabric back (fig. 32). Stitch with small hemming stitches.

Grandmother's Fan quilt

TECHNIQUES: hand piecing; machine piecing; hand quilting; general

	Wall quilt	Single	Double	King-size
Size when completed	92 cm x 1,29 m (37 in. x 52 in.)	1,64 m x 2,35 m (66 in. x 92 in.)	2 m x 2,35 m (80 in. x 95 in.)	2,7 m x 2,35 m (108 in. x 95 in.)
Layout of blocks	2 x 3	4 x 6	5 x 6	7 x 6
Number of blocks	6	24	30	42
Size of blocks 30 cm (12 in.) x 30 cm (12 in.)				
Materials				
variety of fabric remnants	70 cm (¾ yd)	2 m (2¼ yds)	3 m (3½ yds)	3,2 m (3¾ yds)
background fabric	70 cm (¾ yd)	3 m (3½ yds)	3,6 m (4 yds)	4,5 m (5 yds)
fabric for framing strips and first border strip (yellow)	80 cm (⅞ yd)	1,7 m (2 yds)	2,2 m (2½ yds)	4,5 m (5 yds)
fabric for second border strip (pink)	50 cm (⅝ yd)	1 m (1⅓ yd)	1,1 m (1⅝ yd)	1,5 m (1¾ yd)
fabric for backing	1,5 m (1¾ yd)	5 m (5½ yds)	5 m (5½ yds)	7 m (8 yds)
batting	1 m (1⅓ yd)	3,5 m (4 yds)	4 m (4½ yds)	5 m (5½ yds)
pattern (page 122)				

- Cut out the pattern pieces from the fabric remnants.
- Join the pieces for the fan, either by hand or by machine.
- Join the curve to the fan part.
- Cut out a 31,2 cm (12½ in.) x 31,2 cm (12½ in.) block from the background fabric and appliqué the fan design onto it. Complete all the blocks.
- Cut 6,7 cm (2⅝ in.) wide strips from the yellow fabric and join the blocks with the strips in between (page 26).
- Cut out a 10,7 cm (4 ¼ in.) wide border strip from the yellow fabric and sew it right around the joined top.
- Cut out another 8,7 cm (3½ in.) wide border strip from the pink fabric and join it around the yellow strip.
- Trace the quilt pattern onto the top layer. A flower design was quilted on the background fabric of each block and a chain design on the border strips.
- Place the top layer on the batting and the backing. Tack.
- Quilt the design.
- Fold the border strip over, fold in a hem and stitch with small hemming stitches (page 34).

This quilt consists of blocks of which some are divided in half to form triangles. The colours of some of the triangles and squares are arranged to form fish. They are joined with the machine.

Fish and shell motifs are cut from fabric and appliquéd onto the background for an even more striking effect.

Thread in interesting multicoloured shades is used for the machine appliqué. This gives the outline stitching a subtler effect and the colours blend more effectively with the motifs.

TECHNIQUES: machine piecing; machine quilting; hand quilting; general

	Wall quilt	Single	Three-quarter	Double
Size when completed	1,3 m x 1,3 m (52 in. x 52 in.)	1,3 m x 2,06 m (52 in. x 82 in.)	1,7 m x 2,06 m (68 in. x 82 in.)	2,06 m x 2,06 m (82 in. x 82 in.)
Suggested layout of quilt: Centre strip consisting of 6 cm (2⅜ in.) x 6 cm (2⅜ in.) blocks:				
Number of blocks	13 x 13	13 x 24	18 x 24	24 x 24
Width of border strips:				
first dark blue	3 cm (1¼ in.)	6 cm (2⅜ in.)	6 cm (2⅜ in.)	6 cm (2⅜ in.)
light blue	12 cm (4⅞ in.)	16 cm (6⅜ in.)	18 cm (7 in.)	18 cm (7 in.)
second dark blue	4 cm (1½ in.)	6 cm (2⅜ in.)	6 cm (2⅜ in.)	6 cm (2⅜ in.)
Materials fabric with shell and fish motifs				
variety of fabric remnants	1,4 m (1½ yd)	3 m (3½ yds)	3,5 m (4 yds)	3,8 m (4½ yds)
dark-blue fabric for border strips	40 cm (½ yd)	60 cm (¾ yd)	70 cm (¾ yd)	80 cm (⅞ yd)
blue print fabric for border strip	1,2 m (1¼ yd)	1,5 m (1⅞ yd)	1,6 m (1⅞ yd)	1,8 m (2 yds)
fabric for framing	60 cm (¾ yd)	70 cm (⅞ yd)	80 cm (⅞ yd)	1 m (1⅓ yd)
fabric for backing	2 m (2¼ yds)	3,5 m (4 yds)	4,2 m (4¾ yds)	4,5 m (5yds)
batting	1,4 m (1½ yd)	2,3 m (2½ yds)	2,8 m (3 yds)	4 m (4½ yds)
pattern (page 123)				

Fabric with shell or fish motifs was used for appliqué stitches in the blocks and on the border strip.

Enlarge or reduce the quilt by making the centre part larger or smaller, and by making the border strips narrower or broader.

Note: The instructions below are for making the three-quarter quilt. Adjust the measurements and directions for other sizes.

● The easiest way is to draw the quilt on graph paper and to colour it in according to the fabric you have. (The scale could be 1 cm [½ in.] = 6 cm [3 in.].)
● Mark the parts where you intend placing large squares with appliquéd motifs, then you do not have to make 6 cm (3 in.) squares.

● The quilt has 18 blocks on the width and 24 blocks in the length. Divide some of the blocks in half to form fish (fig. 36a and b).
● Place eight squares with fish appliquéd on them on the background fabric. The sizes of the squares are: three of 12 cm (4⅝ in.) x 12 cm (4⅝ in.); three of 18 cm (7⅛ in.) x 18 cm (7⅛ in.), and two of 36 cm (14¼ in.) x 36 cm (14¼ in.). This includes the blue frame. Adjust the sizes as you wish.
● Complete the machine appliqué on the squares, stitch the frame, and join it between the background blocks according to your pattern on graph paper. Use the photograph as a guide.

● Cut a 7,2 cm (2⅞ in.) wide border strip and join around the previous part. Allow the triangles to overlap the border strip for a striking effect.

● Now cut out a 19,2 cm (7¾ in.) wide framing strip and join it to the dark-blue strip. Cut out the fish and shell motifs and machine appliqué onto the background.

● Cut out another 7,2 cm (2⅞ in.) wide dark-blue fabric strip and join.

● Place the top layer on the batting and the backing. Tack or pin to secure.

● Outline quilt the fish by hand.

● Machine quilt the background in flowing lines.

● Cut out a 6 cm (2½ in.) wide fabric strip to serve as the final border finish.

● Place right sides together against the raw edges of the quilt. Stitch through all the layers.

● Fold in a 7 mm (¼ in.) hem and fold half the fabric back (fig. 33). Stitch with small hemming stitches.

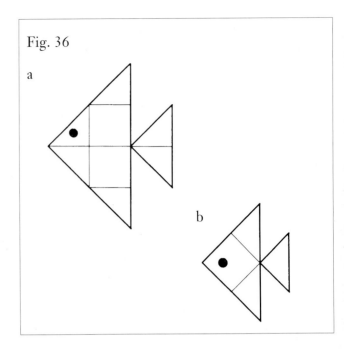

Fig. 36

a

b

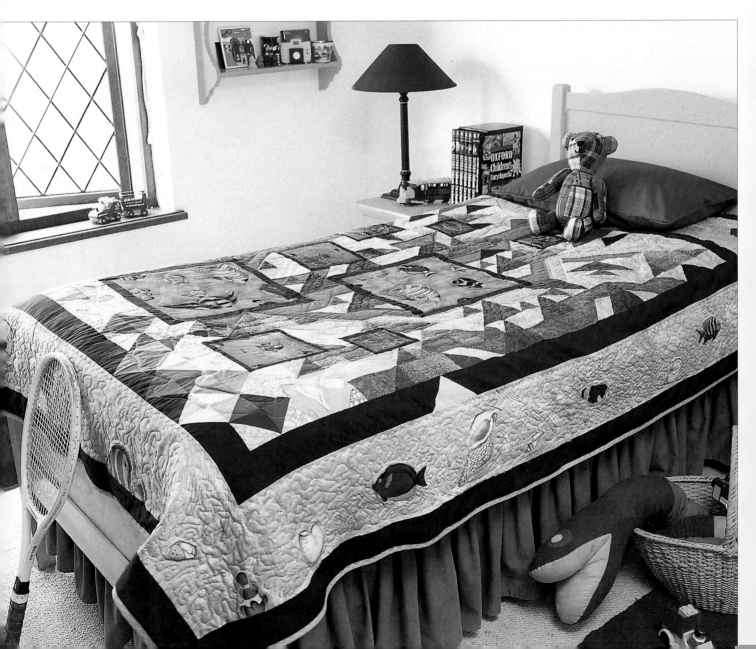

Windmill quilt and Patchwork waistcoat

The Windmill quilt and Patchwork waistcoat are both made of fabric remnants. The waistcoat consists of remnants from men's clothing – especially suits. The waistcoat may be worn with different trousers and can look either formal or informal. It is suitable for men or women. If you intend making a woman's waistcoat, use more embroidery and pretty buttons. The waistcoat can be made to be reversible.

For the Windmill quilt, a simple template is repeated. Eight pattern parts form a square, which forms a windmill pattern. The quilt is made in earthy colours, such as brown, rust, sand and blue. For joining, use your machine or the inlay method.

Windmill quilt

TECHNIQUES: inlay method or machine piecing; quilting; general

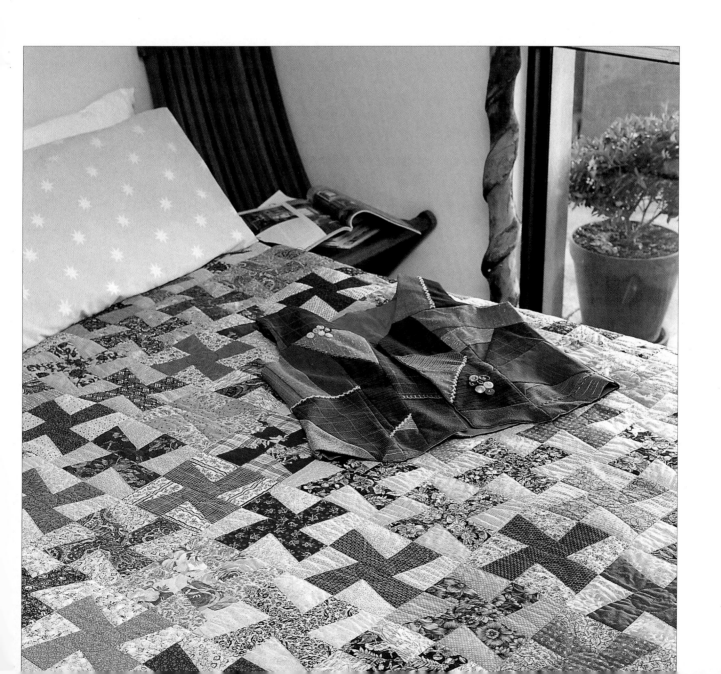

Windmill quilt	Wall quilt	Single	Double	King-size
Size when completed	61 cm x 91 cm (24 in. x 36 in.)	1,4 m x 2 m (56 in. x 82 in.)	2,15 m x 2,15 m (88 in. x 88 in.)	2,45 m x 2,15 m (96 in. x 88 in.)
Layout of blocks	3 x 5	8 x 12	13 x 13	15 x 13
Total number of blocks	15	96	169	195
Size of blocks 15 cm (6 in.) x 15 cm (6 in.)				
Materials				
variety of fabric remnants	1 m (1⅓ yd.)	3 m (3½ yds)	6 m (7 yds)	8 m (9 yds)
fabric for 3 cm (1¼ in.) wide border strip	30 cm (⅜ yd)	50 cm (½ yd)	60 cm (¾ yd)	60 cm (¾ yd)
fabric for 5 cm (2 in.) border strip	40 cm (½ yd)	50 cm (¾ yd)	60 cm (¾ yd)	70 cm (⅞ yd)
fabric for 7 cm (2⅞ in.) wide border strip	40 cm (½ yd)	1 m (1⅓ yd)	1 m (1⅓ yd)	1,3 m (1½ yd)
fabric for binding	40 cm (½ yd)	60 cm (¾ yd)	70 cm (⅞ yd)	70 cm (⅞ yd)
fabric for backing	1 m (1⅓ yd)	2,5 m (3 yds)	5 m (5¾ yds)	7 m (8 yds)
batting	70 cm (⅞ yd)	2 m (2½ yds)	3,5 m (4 yds)	5 m (5¾ yds)
pattern (page 123)				

Choose fabrics for a bold contrast between the pattern pieces in the blocks, for example four light and four dark colours.

Join the pieces with your machine or according to the inlay method (page 14).

● Use the photograph as a guide. Join one light and one dark piece to form a square.
● Repeat with the other six pieces so that you have three squares. Stitch the squares in pairs to form two rectangles.
● Stitch the two rectangles to form one large square.
● Repeat until you have the right number of blocks.
● Join the blocks to form strips as required for the respective quilt sizes.
● Join the strips to complete the quilt top.
● Add seam allowances to the border strips and cut them out of different fabrics.
● Join the narrow border strip all around the outer edges of the blocks.
● Join the second border strip around the first.
● Place the quilt top on the batting and the backing. Tack.
● Apply outline quilting all around the windmills. Sew quilting stitches on the border strips if you wish.
● Cut out a 5 cm (2 in.) wide strip of fabric for the final framing and place right sides facing on the quilt top.
● Stitch it 1 cm (½ in.) from the edge. Fold the fabric over. Fold in a hem and stitch with slip hemming stitches to form an edge of about 1 cm (½ in.).

Patchwork waistcoat

TECHNIQUES: machine or hand patchwork; embroidery; general

MATERIALS
bought waistcoat pattern
fabric remnants (according to pattern)
lining fabric (according to pattern)
embroidery wool and thread (optional)
buttons

● Use a bought pattern as the basis for making the waistcoat.
● Cut the lining from the pattern. If you wish to make it reversible, the lining must be appropriate, for example linen or thicker fabric, not satin.
● Join fabric pieces of various shapes and sizes by hand or with your machine to resemble crazy patchwork.
● Iron the fabric.
● Place the pattern on the fabric and cut out. Decorate the fabric with embroidery stitches if preferred.
● Place together the fabric and lining pieces of the waistcoat with right sides facing and stitch right around, leaving the shoulder seams open.
● Turn right side out.
● Place the shoulder seams of the top layer together and stitch.
● Fold the seam allowance of the shoulder seams of the lining to the inside and stitch with small stitches.
● Decorate the waistcoat with buttons and beads if preferred.

Scrap quilt, Cottage wall quilt and Teddy bears

Fabric remnants were used for all these articles. It is the perfect solution for using all the remnants in your cupboard.

The two teddy bears have different patterns. One is made of pieces of denim (there are even pieces cut from old clothing).

The other bear is made up mainly of pieces of check fabric.

Teddy bears are everyone's favourite and make excellent gifts for people of any age. The fact that you used remnants from old clothing could add to its sentimental value.

The template for the Scrap quilt is one which many people like using, since it can be arranged in various sequences to look completely different each time.

The Cottage quilt will look good in a hallway. You could even embroider the word WELCOME on it.

Scrap quilt

TECHNIQUES: inlay method; hand quilting; general

Scrap quilt				
	Wall quilt	**Single**	**Double**	**King-size**
Size when completed	1 m x 1 m	1,35 m x 2,05 m	2,1 m x 2,1 m	2,4 m x 2,4 m
	(40 in. x 40 in.)	(54 in. x 82 in.)	(84 in. x 84 in.)	(95 in. x 95 in.)
Total number of pieces	168	468	728	990
Materials				
variety of fabric remnants	2 m (2¼ yds)	4,5 m (5 yds)	7,5 m (8½ yds)	8,5 m (9½ yds)
fabric for first border strip	30 cm (⅜ yd)	50 cm (⅝ yd)	60 cm (¾ yd)	80 cm (⅞ yd)
fabric for second border strip	50 cm (⅝ yd)	1 m (1⅓ yd)	1,2 m (1½ yd)	1,5 m (1¾yd)
fabric for backing	1 m (1⅓ yd)	3 m (3½ yds)	5 m (5¾ yds)	6 m (7 yds)
batting	1 m (1⅓ yd)	2,2 m (2½ yds)	4 m (4¾ yds)	4,5 m (5 yds)
pattern (page 123)				

Fabric remnants were used for this quilt. Remnants may be odd pieces, or some may be repeated, depending on the fabric you have at hand. You should, however, distinguish between light and dark fabric colours. For example, arrange light and dark colours to form a specific pattern. Arrange them from light to dark, or begin with dark in the centre and arrange them to grow increasingly lighter towards the outer edge. Or, as in the case of the quilt on the sofa, the rows are made up of different shades of colours. Medium light colours were used in the centre to form a square. This was followed by a darker strip running in a circle, followed by another medium light strip and then a light strip. The strips were repeated to form a pattern running in a circle.

● Follow the instructions for the inlay method (page 14).
● Tack all the fabric pieces over the templates and lay them out so that you can decide on a colour pattern. (Another method is to draw the quilt on paper and to colour it in to correspond with the fabric you have available.)
● Stitch all the pieces together with small topsewing stitches and complete the entire top of the quilt like that.
● Cut out a 4,2 cm (1⅝ in.) wide border strip and join all around the outer edge.

● Cut out another 11,2 cm (4½ in.) wide border strip and join to the previous border strip.
● Place the top layer with right side up on the batting and the backing. Tack the three layers to secure.
● The article is now ready for quilting.
● Fold in a 6 mm (2⅜ in.) hem in the border strip and fold a 2 cm (⅞ in.) edge (⅞ in.) to the back. Stitch with hemming stitches.

Cottage wall quilt

TECHNIQUES: machine patchwork; hand quilting; general

Size when completed 66 cm (26 in.) x 80 cm (32 in.)
Layout of blocks 4 x 5
Total number of blocks 20
Size of blocks 10 cm (4 in.) x 10 cm (4 in.)

MATERIALS
variety of fabric remnants 1 m (1⅓ yd)
fabric for first border strip 30 cm (½ yd)
fabric for second border strip 40 cm (½ yd)
fabric for backing 60 cm (¾ yd)
batting (1,5 m [1¾ yd] wide) 50 cm (½ yd)
bias binding for framing 4 m (4¾ yds)
pattern (page 123)

● Stitch the pattern pieces and complete the block for one cottage.
● Complete all the blocks.
● Cut out 5 cm (2 in.) x 5 cm (2 in.) squares.
● Cut out 5 cm (2 in.) wide strips and join the blocks with sashing and squares in between.
● Cut out a 7 cm (3 in.) wide framing strip and sew around the pieced top.
● Place the top layer on the batting and the backing. Tack.
● Cut a 5 cm (2 in.) border strip and stitch.
● Fold the border strip over and stitch.

Teddy bears

Joints for teddy bears
The joints each consist of a split pin, two washers and two round hardboard discs of about 4 cm (1¾ in.) in diameter.

If the hardboard discs are unobtainable, cut out stiff cardboard and glue two or three together. Unfortunately in this case the teddy bear will not be washable, since the cardboard will soften in water. Plastic discs are also available at some craft shops.

Drill or make holes in the centre of the discs to insert the split pins (if they do not already have holes). Decide where the arms and legs must be attached to the body. Insert the split pin through a washer and a disc. Make a hole in the fabric of the limb and insert the split pin through the fabric – the washer and disc will not pull through. Make a hole in the body and insert the split pin from the limb through the hole and then through a disc and washer again. Bend the ends of the split pin open so that the joint is secure (fig. 37).

Eyes
The position of the eyes is not indicated on the pattern because the eyes are placed according to personal preference. (A teddy bear's eyes are usually quite far apart. Do not place them too high.)

Complete the head and stuff temporarily. Place the eyes on the front of the head to determine the position and make marks to indicate where they must come. Remove the stuffing and place the eyes in position by pressing the pin of each eye through the fabric and pushing the washer in at the back.

Nose

Black wool or six-strand embroidery thread is generally used for a teddy bear's nose. The nose is attached after the head has been stuffed.

Make a knot in the thread. Insert the needle exactly in the centre of the nose position and draw it out at the bottom in the centre. Insert the needle to the left at the top and draw it out under the centre. Insert the needle at the top to the right and draw it out at the bottom in the centre so that it forms a V-shape (fig. 38a).

Fill the entire area with stitches. Sew stitches at the top (fig. 38b) and insert the needle under the V (end of nose).

Sew one straight stitch in the centre down the middle and two slanted stitches for the mouth (fig. 38c).

Check teddy bear

TECHNIQUES: general

MATERIALS
check fabric remnants
2 eyes, 12 mm (½ in.) in diameter
4 split pins
8 hardboard discs, about 4 cm (1½ in.) in diameter
8 washers
black embroidery thread or wool
polyester filling
pattern (pages 124 and 125)

● Join the fabric remnants until you have a large enough piece to cut out all the pattern pieces.
● Cut out the pattern pieces from the fabric.
● Place the ears in pairs with right sides together and stitch to the outer edge.
● Turn right side out. Fold the seam allowance in at the bottom edge, press a little polyester filling in and stitch.
● Place together the two side pieces of the head with right sides facing. Stitch from A to B.
● Stitch the darts on the insert and side pieces.
● Place the insert between the two side pieces with right sides facing. Stitch both sides.
● Turn right side out.
● Place the eyes in position (page 59).
● Place together the front pieces of the body with right sides facing.
● Place together the back pieces right sides facing and stitch the centre front seam. Stitch the centre back seam.
● Place together the front and back of the body right sides together. Stitch the side seams, leaving an

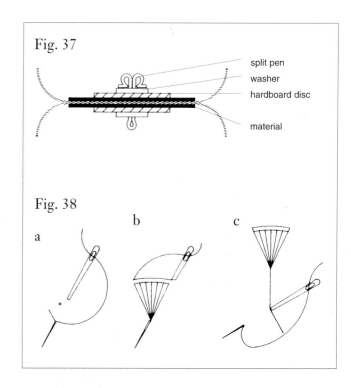

Fig. 37

split pen
washer
hardboard disc
material

Fig. 38

a
b
c

opening of about 10 cm along one side.
● Place the head in the body part with right sides facing. Make sure the centre front seam of the body and the front of the head correspond exactly. Stitch right around. Turn right side out.
● Place the ears in position and stitch with small stitches.
● Place together the arm pieces right sides facing and stitch, leaving an opening at the top ends. Turn right side out.
● Place together the leg pieces right sides facing and stitch from one bottom edge right around up to the other bottom edge, leaving an opening at the top.
● Place the foot soles in the bottom openings with right sides facing and stitch. Turn right side out.
● Place one arm in position. Insert a split pin through a washer and one hardboard disc and place it inside the body where the arm must be. Place the other disc on the inside of the inner arm and insert the ends of the split pin through the disc and a washer. Bend the ends over. Repeat with the other arm.
● Place one leg in position. Insert a split pin through a washer and a hardboard disc and place inside the body where the leg must be. Place the other disc on the inside of the inner leg and insert the ends of the split pin through the disc and a washer. Bend the ends back. Repeat with the other leg.
● Fill the body and stitch the opening at the side.
● Fill the legs and arms and stitch the openings carefully.
● Embroider the nose and mouth with black embroidery thread or wool.

Denim teddy bear

TECHNIQUES: general

MATERIALS
denim fabric remnants
2 eyes, 12 mm (½ in.) in diameter
2 split pins
4 hardboard discs, about 4 cm (1½ in.) in diameter
4 washers
polyester filling
black embroidery thread or wool
pattern (pages 126 and 127)

● Cut the pattern pieces from the denim remnants.
● Place the ears in pairs with right sides facing. Stitch up to the outer edge. Turn right side out and stuff lightly.
● Place together the front pieces of the head with right sides facing and stitch the centre front seam.
● Place together the muzzle and the curve of the front of the head right sides facing. Stitch.
● Fold the front and the muzzle right sides facing and stitch the centre front seam up to the neck line.
● Stitch the ears in position (folded back and flush with raw edges).
● Place together the back pieces right sides facing and stitch the centre back seam.
● Place together the front and back pieces of the head right sides facing and fold the ears to the inside. Stitch from the neckline right around and back to the neckline.

● Place together the parts of the arm pieces right sides facing and stitch, leaving an opening at the top. Turn right side out and stuff the arms.
● Place together the front pieces of the body right sides facing and stitch the centre front seam.
● Place together the back pieces of the body right sides facing and stitch the centre back seam.
● Place the arms about 2 cm (1 in.) from the neckline in position between the front and back pieces and stitch the front and back pieces with right sides facing. Leave an opening on one side for stuffing the body.
● Place the head in the body part with right sides facing and stitch at the neck. Turn right side out.
● Place together the leg pieces right sides facing. Stitch from the one bottom edge right around up to the other bottom edge, leaving an opening at the top.
● Place the foot soles in the openings at the bottom with right sides facing and stitch. Turn right side out.
● Place the legs in position. Insert a split pin through a washer and one hardboard disc. Place inside the body where the leg must be.
● Place the other disc on the inside of the inner leg and insert the ends of the split pin through the disc and a washer. Bend the ends back. Repeat with the other leg.
● Place the eyes in position and attach.
● Stuff the head and body and stitch the opening neatly. Stuff the legs and stitch the openings.
● Embroider the nose and mouth with black embroidery thread or wool.

Blackford's Beauty quilt

TECHNIQUES: machine piecing; hand quilting; general

This quilt consists of 30 cm (12 in.) x 30 cm (12 in.) blocks. It is subdivided into squares, diamonds and triangles, joined with a machine.

The quilt may also be joined with strip piecing. Strips of 3,75 cm (1½ in.) plus seam allowances (thus 4,95 cm/2 in.) must be cut with a rotary cutter and joined. These are subdivided again and joined.

● Cut out the pattern pieces of the required number of blocks from the fabric. Join the pattern pieces as follows:
● Join pieces 1 to 4 to form a small square. Join piece 5 to this square.
● Join pieces 6 and 7 and then join this to the previous part. Repeat with the corresponding pieces.
● Join pieces 8 and 9 to piece 10 and repeat with the mirror image part. Join the two parts. Repeat with the corresponding parts.
● Join the different parts in rows to complete the block.
● Complete the required number of blocks.
● Cut out a 31,2 cm (13 in.) long and 5 cm (2 in.) wide strip of fabric.
● Cut out 5 cm x 5 cm squares and join to the strips. Use these as frames between the blocks. Use the photograph as a guide and complete the quilt top.
● Cut out a 5 cm (2 in.) wide blue border strip and join.
● Cut out a 10 cm (4 in.) wide light-coloured print fabric and join.
● Place the top layer on the batting and the backing. Tack. Quilt the article.
● Cut out a 6 cm (2½ in.) wide binding and fold in half over the length. Stitch.
● Follow the instructions for double binding on page 33 and complete the article.

Blackford's Beauty quilt	Wall quilt	Single	Double	King-size
Size when completed	1,16 m x 1,16 m (46 in. x 46 in.)	1,47 m x 1,81 m (58 in. x 72 in.)	2 m x 2,34 m (80 in. x 93 in.)	2,68 m x 2,68 m (105 in. x 105 in.)
Layout of blocks	3 x 3	4 x 6	5 x 6	7 x 7
Number of blocks	9	24	30	49
Materials				
first blue fabric (squares)	40 cm (½ yd)	1,2 m (1⅜ yd)	1,5 m (1¾ yd)	2,5 m (2¾ yds)
second blue fabric (diamonds)	60 cm (¾ yd)	1,4 m (1½ yd)	1,7 m (2 yds)	2,8 m (3½ yds)
light-coloured fabric for background	1,2 m (1⅜ yd)	2,7 m (3¼ yds)	3,5 m (4 yds)	5,5 m (6¼ yds)
fabric for blue border strip, 3,8 cm (1½ in.) wide	40 cm (½ yd)	60 cm (¾ yd)	70 cm (¾ yd)	90 cm (1 yd)
fabric for light-coloured print fabric border strip of 8,8 cm (3½ in.) wide	80 cm (⅞ yd.)	90 cm (1 yd)	1,3 m (1½ yd)	1,6 m (1⅞ yd)
fabric for binding, about 2 cm (1 in.) wide	40 cm (½ yd)	70 cm (¾ yd)	1,1 m (1⅜ yd)	1,5 m (1¾ yd)
fabric for backing	1,5 m (1¾ yd)	2,2 m (2½ yds)	4,8 m (5¾ yds)	7 m (7¾ yds)
batting	1,2 m (1⅜ yd)	2 m (2¼ yds)	4,8 m (5¾ yds)	5,4 m (6¼ yds)
pattern (page 128)				

Blue-and-white Log Cabin quilt

TECHNIQUES: folded-over method; machine quilting; general

One half of each block is composed of a light-coloured fabric, while the other half is composed of a dark-coloured fabric. Sort your fabric remnants into light and dark colours. Contrasting fabric may also be used, for example pink and green.

The fastest method of assembling this quilt is to draw the pattern for one block on paper and to make photocopies of it. Make as many photocopies of the pattern as the number of blocks you need. Stitch the fabric strips to these paper foundations according to the folded-over method. The paper-based method can also be used. Stitch the fabric strips to the wrong side of the paper (page 18). Remove the paper once the blocks have been joined.

● Cut all the fabric, except for the border strip and binding, into 2,5 cm (1 in.) wide strips plus a 6 mm (¼ in.) seam allowance on both sides, thus 3,7 cm (1½ in.) wide.
● Follow the folded-over method (page 15) and complete all the blocks.

● Join the completed blocks. The blocks may be arranged in several ways (fig. 5a, b and c).
● Begin at the top row and stitch the blocks at the side seams to form a long strip.
● Repeat with subsequent rows until all the blocks are in strips.
● Now join the long strips. Make sure the seam lines correspond exactly.
● If you used papers, remove them now.
● Sew the 8,2 cm (3¼ in.) wide border strip around the pieced top.
● Tack the top layer onto the batting and the backing.
● Quilt as preferred, for example circle motifs or outline quilting.
● Cut out 60 cm (24 in.) strips for the binding. Follow the instructions for one of the edge finishing methods on pages 33 and 34.

Trip around the World quilt

Follow the instructions for making the quilt on page 78.

Blue-and-white Log Cabin quilt	Wall quilt	Single	Double	King-size
Size when completed	1,15 m x 1,15 m (45 in. x 45 in.)	1,50 m x 2,03 m (60 in. x 81 in.)	2,20 m x 2,20 m (88 in. x 88 in.)	2,55 m x 2,37 m (102 in. x 94 in.)
Layout of blocks	6 x 6	8 x 11	12 x 12	14 x 13
Total number of blocks	36	88	144	182
Materials				
variety of fabric remnants	3 m (3½ yds)	5 m (6 yds)	8 m (9 yds)	9 m (10 yds)
fabric for 7 cm (2¾ in.) wide border strip	60 cm (¾ yd)	80 cm (⅞ yd)	1 m (1⅓ yd)	1,2 m (1⅜ yd)
fabric for backing	1,5 m (1¾ yd)	4 m (4¾ yds)	4,5 m (5 yds)	6,5 m (7¼ yds)
batting	1,2 m (1⅜ yd)	2,2 m (2½ yds)	4 m (4¾ yds)	5 m (5½ yds)
binding	50 cm (½ yd)	60 cm (¾ yd)	90 cm (1 yd)	1,2 m (1⅜ yd)

Charm quilt

This quilt is also called the Thousand pyramids.

TECHNIQUES: inlay method; hand quilting; general

This quilt is assembled from fabric remnants which are all different.
● Cut out the required number of pieces from the fabric.
● Follow the instructions for the inlay method and tack all the pieces over paper templates.
● Lay the pieces out and decide how you want the colours assembled. The pieces may be laid out to form diamonds, a star, or large triangles. The different colours, as well as the colour value (light and dark), will influence the appearance of the quilt.
● Stitch the pieces in rows.
● Stitch the rows to complete the top layer.
● Cut out two 12 cm (5 in.) wide border strips and stitch the two straight sides to these.
● Cut out two more border strips, each 17 cm (6 in.) wide, and stitch the two asymmetrical rows to these.
● Quilt patterns of your choice on the top layer.
● Place the top layer on the batting and the backing. Tack securely.
● Quilt the article as you wish.
● Fold the border strip over. Fold in a small hem and stitch to the back with small hemming stitches.

Charm quilt	Wall quilt	Single	Double	King-size
Size when completed	1 m x 1 m (40 in. x 40 in.)	1,4 m x 2,06 m (55 in. x 82 in.)	2,2 m x 2,06 m (88 in. x 82 in.)	2,4 m x 2,2 m (96 in. x 88 in.)
Total number of pieces	190	621	1 035	1 225
Materials				
variety of fabric remnants	2 m (2¼ yds)	4,5 m (5 yds)	7 m (7¾ yds)	9 m (10 yds)
fabric for border strip	80 cm (⅞ yd)	1,5 m (1¾ yd)	2 m (2¼ yds)	2,2 m (2½ yds)
fabric for backing	1,1 m (1¼ yd)	3 m (3½ yds)	4,5 m (5 yds)	5,5 m (6¼ yds)
batting	1 m (1⅓ yd)	2,2 m (2½ yds)	4 m (4¾ yds)	4,5 m (5 yds)
pattern (page 128)				

Log Cabin quilt with black block frames and Four-Patch quilt

The Log Cabin quilt on the bench differs from the traditional Log Cabin pattern.

Each block has a black framing and starts with a small black square. Some of the black squares are positioned in the corner, with material strips stitched along two sides. Squares in the other blocks are placed in the middle with material strips stitched around it.

The beautiful Four-Patch quilt has two different blocks which are joined alternately. This creates the impression of big squares with small squares in the centre.

Log Cabin quilt with black block frames	Wall quilt	Single	Double	King-size
Size when completed	1,2 m x 1,2 m (48 in. x 48 in.)	1,6 m x 2 m (64 in. x 48 in.)	2 m x 2 m (80 in. x 80 in.)	2,7 m x 2,35 m (108 in. x 93 in.)
Layout of blocks	6 x 6	8 x 10	10 x 10	14 x 12
Total number of blocks	36	80	100	168
Materials				
variety of fabrics in different colours	3 m (3½ yds)	5 m (5½ yds)	8 m (9 yds)	9 m (10 yds)
black fabric	1,4 m (1¾ yd)	2,2 m (2½ yds)	3 m (3½ yds)	4 m (4¾ yds)
fabric for backing	1,5 m (1¾ yd)	4 m (4¾ yds)	5 m (5½ yds)	6 m (6¾ yds)
batting	1,5 m (1¾ yd)	2,2 m (2½ yds)	4 m (4¾ yds)	6 m (6¾ yds)
pattern (page 135)				

Log Cabin quilt with black block frames

Although it does not take long to make this quilt, it is very striking because all the blocks are made differently.

TECHNIQUES: folded-over method; machine piecing; hand quilting; general

This quilt has an interesting colour combination of green, peach, cream, black, orange and burgundy. The quilt in the sketch (page 135) is for a double bed. In this quilt there are three blocks close to each corner, which are made differently from the other blocks. The black squares of these blocks are placed in the corners instead of in the centre.

If you intend making a quilt in any of the other sizes, it is better first to draw the blocks and to decide how you want to assemble them.

Colour in the pattern according to the colours of your fabric to determine where you want the light and the dark colours.

● Cut the black fabric in 4,2 cm (1¾ in.) wide strips for the centre blocks. Subdivide these strips of fabric to form 4,2 cm (1¾ in.) x 4,2 cm (1¾ in.) squares.
● Cut 3 cm (1¼ in.) wide strips out of the coloured fabric.
● Place the black squares in position. Join the strips all around as in figure 4.
● Complete the required number of these blocks.
● For the blocks where the black squares are placed in the corners, the coloured strips must be stitched to two sides only. Complete the required number of these blocks.
● Arrange the blocks in the pattern of your choice.
● Cut out 3 cm (1¼ in.) wide strips of black fabric and join the blocks with the black strips in between.
● Place the top layer on the batting and the backing. Quilt the article.
● Make a 7 cm (2⅞ in.) wide black border strip and finish the edge according to one of the methods on page 33.

Four-Patch quilt

	Wall quilt	Single	Double	King-size
Size when completed	1,14 m x 1,14 m (45 in. x 45 in.)	1,7 m x 2,12 m 68 in. x 83½ in.)	2,12 m x 2,12 m (83½ in. x 83½ in.)	2,4 m x 2,26 m (96 in. x 90 in.)
Number of blocks with squares	9	35	49	56
Number of blocks with triangles	4	24	36	42
Number of half-blocks with triangles	8	20	24	26
Size of blocks 14 cm (5½ in.) x 14 cm (5½ in.)	4	4	4	4
Materials				
variety of fabric remnants	80 cm (⅞ yd)	3,5 m 4 yds)	4,8 m (5¾ yds)	5,8 m (6½ yds)
blue fabric	40 cm (½ yd)	1,2 m (1½ yd)	1,8 m (2 yds)	2,2 m (2½ yds)
light-coloured fabric	20 cm (¼ yd)	1 m (1⅓ yd)	1,4 m (1¾ yd)	1,8 m (2 yds)
red fabric for border strips	60 cm (¾ yd)	1 m (1⅓ yd)	1,2 m (1½ yd)	1,4 m (1¾ yd)
material for binding	40 cm (½ yd)	60 cm (¾ yd)	80 cm (⅞ yd)	90 cm (1 yd)

Four-Patch quilt

TECHNIQUES: strip piecing; machine piecing; hand quilting; general

To achieve the same effect as the quilt in the photograph, the fabric for the block with the triangles should consist of boldly contrasting colours. The colours of the fabric remnants are mainly medium to dark.

● Cut out 4,7 cm (1⅞ in.) wide strips from the fabric remnants. Join four of the strips lengthwise to form one broad strip. Subdivide this strip into small 4,7 cm (1⅞ in.) wide strips.
● Join four of the strips to form a square with 16 blocks.
● Cut out two blue and two white triangles (piece A) and join to form a square. Complete the number of squares required. Join the squares alternately to form strips, then join the strips.

● Join two small white triangles (piece B) to both sides of a blue triangle (piece A) to form a rectangle, then join a white rectangle to this. Repeat until you have sufficient strips to join right around the blocks. It will now appear as if your blocks are on the diagonal.
● Cut out a red 4 cm (1¾ in.) border strip and join it right around.
● Cut out two white strips and one print fabric strip measuring 5 cm (2 in.) wide. Join the white strips to both sides of the print fabric. Subdivide the strips into smaller 5 cm wide strips and follow the seminole method (fig.10).
● Join the border strip.
● Cut out a red 6 cm (2½ in.) wide border strip and join.
● Place the top layer on the batting and the backing. Tack. Quilt the article.
● Cut out a 6 cm (2½ in.) wide binding and fold it in half over the length. Stitch and follow the directions for the double binding on page 33. Complete the article.

The Amish are a group of people who live in certain parts of America. On a recent visit to Lancaster, Pennsylvania, I found it interesting to see how they live. They are deeply committed to their religion and avoid everything that threatens their religious principles. They shun modern technology, even when they can afford it. Most of them own large farms and houses. The large houses are necessary because they generally have large families. They do not own motor vehicles as they believe in a slow and calm lifestyle. Nor do they use telephones or any electric appliances. It is said that they do not have electricity in their homes as this may tempt them to acquire television sets or radios, thereby exposing their children to the evils of the modern world.

The Amish wear simple clothing fashioned from a standard pattern in a plain colour – usually black and blue. All the women wear their hair with a path in the middle and a bun, and they all wear bonnets.

The Amish do not allow photographs to be taken of them, which is probably the reason why their dolls have no faces.

The Amish women do beautiful needlework and are particularly well known for their beautiful quilts. The quilts in the photographs were made according to traditional colours and patterns.

Amish Nine-Patch quilt

TECHNIQUES: strip piecing; machine piecing; machine or hand quilting

For this quilt the traditional Nine-Patch block was made and joined with green strips and a coloured block in each corner. These blocks are the same size as the Nine-Patch blocks and the narrow strips are the same width. The strips are the same length as the Nine-Patch block.

The completed blocks are stitched diagonally alternating with black blocks.

The quilt may be made according to the strip piecing method or with templates. The strip piecing method is recommended as it is much quicker.

● Cut out 5 cm (2 in.) wide strips with a rotary cutter from the different plain fabrics. Follow the instructions for the strip piecing method on page 16 and complete the centres of the blocks.
● Cut out strips of green fabric the same width as three of the blocks when they are joined (3,8 cm [1½ in.] x 3 blocks = 11,4 cm [4½ in.] + 6 mm [¼ in.] seam allowance at the beginning and end = 12,6 cm [5 in.] wide).
● Join two 5 cm (2 in.) wide strips to both sides of a 12,6 cm (5 in.) wide strip so that it is now 20,2 cm (8 in.) wide. Then subdivide this strip into 5 cm (2 in.) wide strips.

Amish Nine-Patch quilt				
	Wall quilt	**Single**	**Double**	**King-size**
Size when completed	1,12 m x 1,12 m (44 in. x 44 in.)	1,86 m x 1,86 m (74 in. x 74 in.)	2,13 m x 2,13 m (84 in. x 84 in.)	2,4 m x 2,4 m (94 in. x 94 in.)
Number of pieced blocks	9	25	36	49
Number of alternate blocks (black)	4	16	25	36
Number of black triangles	8	16	20	24
Number of triangles at corners of quilt	4	4	4	4
Materials				
variety of plain fabric	1 m (1⅓ yd)	2,4 m (2¾ yds)	4 m (4¾ yds)	5 m (5½ yds)
black fabric	1,2 m (1⅜ yd)	3,3 m (3¾ yds)	4 m (4¾ yds)	4,8 m (5¼ yds)
fabric for green framing strip	80 cm (⅞ yd)	1,1 m (1¼ yd)	1,2 m (1⅜ yd)	1,6 m (1⅞ yd)
fabric for backing	1,5 m (1¾ yd)	4 m (4¾ yds)	4,5 m (5 yds)	5 m (5½ yds)
batting	1 m (1⅓ yd)	3 m (3½ yds)	4 m (4¾ yds)	5 m (5½ yds)

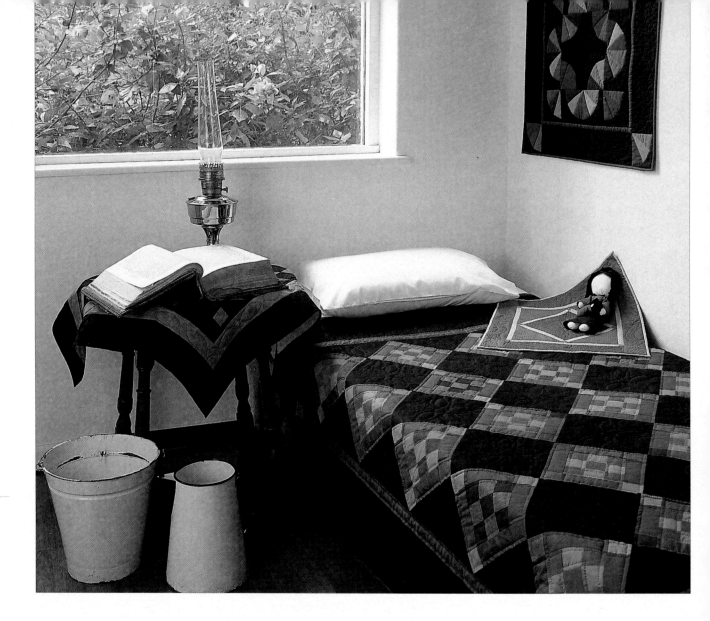

● Take one of the nine-patch blocks and join a 5 cm (2 in.) wide strip of green fabric to form a rectangle.
● Now take one of the fabric strips which you have joined and cut. Join it to both sides of the rectangle to form a square. Use the photograph as a guide.
● Repeat with the number of blocks required.
● Cut out 20,2 cm (8 in.) x 20,2 cm (8 in.) black squares. Sew alternately to the pieced blocks to form strips.
● Cut out 25 cm (10 in.) x 25 cm (10 in.) squares, then cut them diagonally to form two triangles. Join to the ends of the strips (use the photograph as a guide).
● Join the strips (page 27). (The triangles will be slightly too large but may be trimmed once the strips have been joined.)
● Cut out a 32 cm (13 in.) x 32 cm (13 in.) square and cut this diagonally twice to form four triangles. Join them at the corners.
● Trim all excess fabric at the triangles to neaten the article.
● Cut out a 5 cm (2 in.) wide green border strip and

join around the outer edge.
● Cut out a black border strip to the required length and join around the outer edge.
● Transfer the quilting patterns with a white pencil.
● Place the top layer with right sides facing up on the batting and the backing. Tack securely.
● Hand or machine quilt. Quilt a pretty pattern in each black block.
● Cut out a 4 cm (1¾ in.) wide strip of green fabric to serve as the final edge finishing.
● Place this strip with right sides facing against the raw edge of the quilt and stitch through all the layers.
● Place the top layer on the batting and the backing. Stitch.
● Trim the excess batting and backing so that sufficient remains to fill the binding once it has been folded over.
● Fold in a 6 mm (¼ in.) hem and fold half of the fabric strip over. Stitch to the back with small hemming stitches. (Use whichever of the other edge finishing methods you prefer.)

Amish diamond quilt

This small wall quilt was made according to the traditional Amish diamond pattern. Use the same pattern to make a bed quilt. Quilting is important with this type of quilt because of the simplicity of the pattern.

TECHNIQUES: machine patchwork; hand quilting; general

Size of quilt when completed is 50 cm (20 in.) x 50 cm (20 in.)

MATERIALS
40 cm (½ yd) pink fabric
40 cm (½ yd) blue fabric
40 cm (½ yd) purple fabric
60 cm (¾ yd) fabric for the backing
60 cm (¾ yd) batting

● Cut out a 20 cm (8 in.) x 20 cm (8 in.) square for the centre block.
● Cut out four 3 cm (1¼ in.) x 20 cm (8 in.) pink strips of fabric.
● Cut out four 3 cm (1¼ in.) x 3 cm (1¼ in.) purple blocks.
● Join two of the fabric strips to both sides of the centre block.
● Join the small blocks to both sides of the other two strips. Join these to the centre block to form a square again.
● Cut out one 25 cm (10 in.) x 25 cm (10 in.) square from the blue fabric. Divide it diagonally into quarters to form triangles.
● Join the triangles to the previous square to form a square again. (Use the photograph as a guide.) The triangles will be slightly too large, but trim the excess fabric – remember to leave a seam allowance of 6 mm (¼ in.).
● Cut out a pink 3 cm (1¼ in.) border strip and join it around the square.
● Cut out four 6 cm (2½ in.) x 6 cm (2½ in.) blue squares.
● Cut out four purple strips of fabric measuring 6 cm (2½ in.) wide and the same length as the square.
● Join the blue squares to the ends of the purple fabric strips and join around the top layer. (Follow the same method as for the strips and blocks joined around the centre block.)
● Apply a pretty quilting pattern on the top layer.
● Place the top layer with right side up on the batting and the backing. Tack securely.
● Quilt the pattern using tiny stitches.

● Cut out a 5 cm (2 in.) wide strip of pink fabric to serve as the final edge finish.
● Place this strip with right sides facing against the raw edge of the quilt and stitch through all the layers.
● Fold in a 6 mm (¼ in.) hem and fold half of the fabric strip over.
● Stitch to the back with tiny hemming stitches.

Amish Grandmother's Fan wall quilt

TECHNIQUES: machine piecing; hand piecing; machine or hand quilting; general

Size when completed is 65 cm (25½ in.) x 65 cm (25½ in.)
Total number of blocks 20
Size of blocks 10 cm (4 in.) x 10 cm (4 in.)

MATERIALS
variety of fabric remnants
1,4 cm (1¾ yd) black fabric for top layer and backing
0,7 m (¾ yd) batting
pattern (page 129)

● Cut out templates for 20 blocks from the fabric.
● Stitch the pieces for the fan (piece A). (Join by hand or by machine.)
● Stitch the fan to piece B to form a square.
● Join the centre part of the quilt by stitching it in four rows of four blocks each and then joining the four rows. (Use the photograph as a guide.)
● Cut out a 3,2 cm (1¼ in.) wide border strip and stitch it around the outer edge.
● Cut four strips measuring 11,2 cm (4½ in.) wide and 45,2 cm (19 in.) long.
● Join two of the strips to both sides of the centre part to form a rectangle.
● Sew two of the pieced blocks to both sides of each of the remaining two strips and sew to the pieced part to form a square.
● Place the top layer with right side facing up on the batting and the backing. Tack securely.
● Hand or machine quilt.
● Cut out a 4 cm (1¾ in.) wide strip of fabric to serve as the final edge finishing.
● Place this strip with right sides facing against the raw edge of the quilt and stitch through all the layers.
● Fold in a 6 mm (¼ in.) hem and fold half of the fabric strip over.
● Stitch to the back with small hemming stitches.

Hexagon tablecloth, Broderie perse wall hanging, Postage stamp quilt and Starry Path miniature quilt

The colours of these quilted articles lend a warm ambience to a room.

Both the quilt and the tablecloth were made from fabric remnants. The large wall hanging was made of fabric with Jacobean motifs and a peacock. These motifs were cut out and appliquéd onto the background fabric. The tree was enlarged by adding appliquéd flowers to the original motif. Quilting is an important element in this quilt.

The tablecloth was made according to the traditional Grandmother's Flower Garden pattern. It consists of hexagons arranged in rows around a focal point.

The quilt is composed of small blocks and strips combined to form larger blocks. The burgundy and yellow blocks create an impression of steps.

The miniature wall hanging consists of one pattern which is repeated six times. The largest piece is 4 cm.

Hexagon tablecloth

TECHNIQUES: inlay method; general

Size is about 1 m (1⅓ yd) in diameter

MATERIALS
variety of fabric remnants
1,1 m (1¼ yd) fabric for backing
pattern (page 128)

● Follow the instructions for the inlay method on page 14.
● Begin with the first hexagon and join six hexagons all around.
● Now join a row of 12 hexagons. With each row the circle grows bigger and each time there are six more hexagons. In other words, 18, 24, 30, 36, 42, and so on until the last row, which contains 84 hexagons. The total number of hexagons required is therefore 611.
● Enlarge or reduce the tablecloth by joining more or fewer rows. Or enlarge the tablecloth by enlarging the hexagons.

● To attach the backing for the tablecloth, proceed as follows: Unpick all the tacking stitches around the outer edge of the last row of pieces and fold the seam allowance open.
● Place the tablecloth with right sides facing on the backing. Stitch all around the edges where the fold marks are, in other words where the papers end. Leave about three blocks open.
● Trim all excess seam allowances. Remove all the papers and turn right side out through the opening.
● Check whether all the corners are neat and stitch the opening. (An alternative method is to appliqué the pieced top onto a round foundation cloth.)

Broderie perse wall hanging

TECHNIQUES: appliqué; quilting; general

Size of wall hanging is about 1,4 m (56 in.) x 1,3 m (52 in.)

MATERIALS
fabric with suitable motifs
background fabric
fabric for backing
fabric for border strip
fabric for binding
batting
fabric for border strips and framing

The choice of fabric plays an important role in broderie perse appliqué. It should be possible to cut out the motifs on the fabric in order to appliqué them onto the background. Several motifs combined could form a larger pattern. Printed cotton, printed chintz, or finely woven curtain fabric are suitable for this technique. Choose a fabric that does not fray.

● Cut the background fabric to the required size.
● Cut out the motifs from the fabric; remember to add a seam allowance.
● Place the motifs in position on the background fabric. Use one of the appliqué methods on page 19

and stitch the pieces onto the background. Complete the entire design.

- Cut out a border strip, about 5 cm (2 in.) wide, and stitch right around.
- Cut out a strip of about 13 cm (5¼ in.) from the background fabric and stitch.
- Appliqué more motifs on this strip to form a pretty border motif.
- Cut out another border strip, about 6 cm (2⅜ in.) wide, and stitch.
- Mark the quilt patterns on the top layer. (The quilting lines of the tree motif are about 1,2 cm (½ in.) apart. Motifs such as twigs and leaves are also quilted onto the background. Draw motifs to match your design.)
- Place the top layer on the batting and the backing. Tack securely.
- Complete the quilting.
- Cut out a strip of fabric, about 3 cm (1¼ in.) wide, for the binding. Place with right sides facing against the raw edge of the quilt and stitch through all the layers.
- Trim any excess fabric and batting, taking care to have sufficient left to fill the binding strip.
- Fold in a 6 mm (¼ in.) hem. Fold half of the fabric over (page 34). Stitch to the back with small hemming stitches. (Any of the other methods for stitching a binding may be used.)

Postage stamp quilt

Fran Davidtsz made this quilt for her daughter's 21st birthday. She embroidered the following right around the border in stem stitch:

Made with love especially for Kathy on her 21st Birthday on the 22 May.

Life, like your quilt, is made of light and dark patches
Be happy & enjoy the bright times
In dark times, search within yourself
Find God (Luke 17:21) in your centre
Know that together you are strong
Frances Davidtsz 1995 Love Mom

TECHNIQUES: machine piecing; folded-over method; machine or hand quilting; embroidery; general

This quilt is joined virtually the same as a log cabin quilt, except that small blocks are inserted in the corners.

Work out how you wish to arrange the different colours in your quilt. Sort the fabric according to colour and colour value, in other words light and dark.

- Cut the fabric in 3 cm (1¼ in.) wide strips.
- A quick method for making the inside four blocks of each large block is to join a burgundy and a yellow strip. Cut these strips into lengths of 3 cm (1¼ in.) and join two of the strips to form a square.
- Then join the strips in a circle on a foundation cloth or paper (fig. 4). Join first a yellow and burgundy block alternately to the strip that must be joined. The yellow and burgundy corners will run diagonally down the quilt like steps. Use the photograph as a guide.
- A quick method for joining the yellow and burgundy blocks to the strips is as follows: Cut a long strip of yellow and a long strip of burgundy fabric, about 3 cm (1¼ in.) wide. Cut a long strip of fabric

Postage stamp quilt				
	Wall quilt	Single	Double	King-size
Size when completed	95 cm x 1,36 m (38 in. x 55in.)	1,36 m x 2,08 m (55 in. x 83 in.)	2,08 m x 2,46 m (83 in. x 98 in.)	2,46 m x 2,46 m (98 in. x 98 in.)
Layout of blocks	4 x 6	6 x 10	12 x 12	12 x 12
Total number of blocks	24	60	144	144
Size of blocks 18 cm (6¼ in.) x 18 cm (6¼ in.)				
Materials				
variety of fabric remnants	2,5 m (2¾ yds)	5 m (5½ yds)	7,5 m (8¼ yds)	9 m (10 yds)
fabric for border strip	1 m (1⅓ yd)	1,4 m (1¾ yd)	2 m (2¼ yds)	2,2 m (2½ yds)
fabric for binding	30 cm (⅜ yd)	40 cm (½ yd)	60 cm (¾ yd)	90 cm (1 yd)
fabric for backing	1,5 m (1¾ yd)	2,5 m (2⅞ yds)	5 m (5½ yds)	5 m (5½ yds)
batting	1 m (1⅓ yds)	2,2 m (2½ yds)	4,4 m (4⅞ yds)	5 m (5½ yds)
pattern (page 130)				

(for example blue in the required width; 4,4 cm (1⅞ in.) on the pattern). Join the yellow and burgundy fabrics to both sides of the broader strip. Subdivide this into 3 cm (1¼ in.) wide strips. Use such a strip each time as required according to the pattern.
● Arrange the blocks as preferred.
● Stitch the blocks in rows to form strips.
● Stitch all the strips.
● Cut out a 12 cm (4¾ in.) wide border strip and stitch to the quilt.
● Embroider on the border strip if preferred.
● Place the top layer with right side facing up on the batting and the backing. Tack securely.
● Quilt by machine or by hand.
● Cut a 5 cm (2 in.) wide strip of fabric for the binding and place with right sides facing against the raw edge of the quilt.
● Stitch through all the layers.
● Fold in a 6 mm (¼ in.) hem, then fold half the fabric over.
● Stitch to the back with small hemming stitches.

Starry Path miniature quilt

TECHNIQUES: machine piecing; hand quilting; general

Size when completed is 17 cm (7 in.) x 23 cm (9¼ in.)
Layout of blocks 2 x 3
Size of blocks 6 cm (2½ in.) x 6 cm (2½ in.)

MATERIALS
fabric remnants
fabric for border strips
fabric for backing
batting
pattern (page 129)

● Cut out the pattern pieces from the fabric.
● Join the pattern pieces in the following sequence: Join pieces 1 and 2 to both sides of piece 3. Join to piece 4. (Make the block according to the paper-based machine method if preferred. In this case it is divided into four parts, each consisting of pieces 1 to 4.)
● Join the completed blocks.

● Cut out a border strip of about 4 cm (1¼ in.) wide and join around the edge.
● Cut out another 3 cm (1½ in.) wide border strip and join to the edge.
● Place the top layer with the right side facing on the batting and the backing. Tack.
● Quilt the article.
● Fold in a hem of 6 mm (¼ in.), then fold over about 1 cm (½ in.) of the border strip.
● Stitch to the back with small hemming stitches.
● Embroider stem stitches around the first border strip if you wish.

Black-and-white Log Cabin quilt with stars

This is a beautiful quilt for a modern or an old-fashioned bedroom.

It has an interesting combination of black and white. The fine floral fabrics used for the quilt tone down the effect which a black-and-white quilt would normally have.

The quilt is joined by machine according to the folded-over method. An additional diamond-shaped pattern piece is added in the corners to form a star when the blocks are joined.

TECHNIQUES: machine patchwork; folded-over method; hand quilting; general

● Cut out a 4,2 cm (1¾ in.) x 4,2 (1¾ in.) cm centre block for each block.
● Cut out 5 cm (2 in.) wide fabric strips from the light- and dark-coloured fabrics.
● Follow the folded-over method on page 15 and stitch three strips right around on each side.
● Cut out pieces from the black fabric using the diamond-shaped template. Join two black pieces to the ends of the next strip and join the strip so that the black pieces are at the corners. Join another three strips in this way to complete the block.
● Join the blocks.
● Cut out a 6 cm (2½ in.) wide border strip from the first print fabric and sew this around the joined top layer.
● Cut out a 20 cm (8 in.) wide border strip from the second print fabric and join it around the first. (The framing for the wall hanging could be narrower.)
● Place the top layer on the batting and the backing. Tack.
● Quilt the article.
● Cut out a 9,2 cm (3¾ in.) wide strip of black fabric for a double binding, following the instructions on page 33.

	Wall quilt	Single	Double	King-size
Size when completed	1,6 m x 1,6 m	1,7 m x 2 m	2 m x 2,6 m	2,6 m x 2,6 m
Layout of blocks	4 x 4	4 x 6	6 x 7	7 x 7
Total number of blocks	16	24	42	49
Size of blocks 27 cm (10½ in.) x 27 cm (10½ in.)				
Materials				
light-coloured fabric remnants	1 m (1⅓ yd)	2 m (2¼ yds)	3,5 m (4 yds)	4,5 m (5 yds)
dark-coloured fabric remnants	1 m (1⅓ yd)	2 m (2¼ yds)	3,5 m (4 yds)	4,5 m (5 yds)
fabric for second print fabric border strip	70 cm (¾ yd)	70 cm (¾ yd)	1 m (1⅓ yd)	1,2 m (1¼ yd)
fabric for first print fabric border strip	1,5 m (1¾ yd)	1,8 m (2 yds)	2,2 m (2½ yds)	2,5 m (2⅞ yds)
fabric for diamond shapes and framing	80 cm (⅞ yd)	1 m (1⅓ yd)	1,2 m (1⅜ yd)	1,4 m (1¾ yd)
fabric for backing	2 m (2¼ yds)	3,4 m (4 yds)	5 m (5½ yds)	6 m (6¾ yds)
batting	1 m (1⅓ yd)	2,5 m (2¾ yds)	5 m (5½ yds)	6 m (6¾ yds)
pattern (page 129)				

Trip around the World quilt

TECHNIQUES: strip piecing; quilting; general

Size when completed about 2,2 m (88 in.) x 1,28 m (50 in.)

MATERIALS
90 cm (1 yd) each of 7 different fabrics for the blocks
2 m (2¼ yds) fabric for the border strips
3,5 m (4 yds) for the backing fabric
2 m (2½ yds) batting

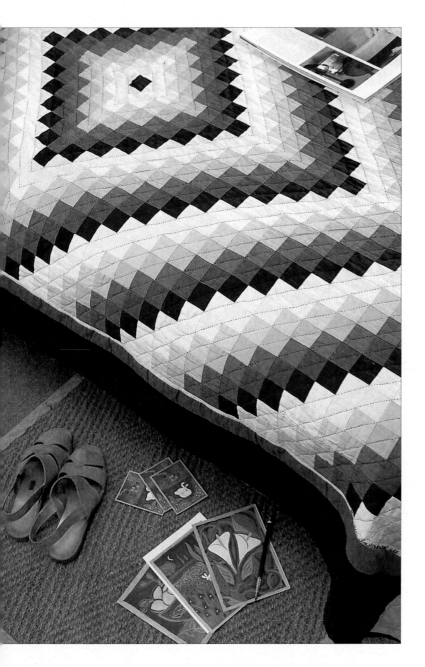

Adjust the size of the quilt by cutting the strips larger or smaller.

The strip piecing machine method (page 16) is an excellent choice for a Trip around the World quilt. It is composed of fabric cut in strips of the same width. The strips are joined so that one of each colour fabric together form a broad strip. In this case the strips were 3,2 cm (1¼ in.) wide plus a 6 mm (¼ in.) seam allowance on both sides, therefore 4,4 cm (1¾ in.) wide.

The strips are subdivided into the same width as the strips were originally cut. When they are joined again, they form squares.

The subdivided strips are joined in "steps". Each time a colour is placed one block lower than the previous one.

An easier method of joining these subdivided strips is to make a round, continuous band of each strip. Join the ends of each strip to form a circle. Unpick the seam at the colour which must come first for the next round. This will save time.

● Draw the quilt on paper and colour it in more or less according to the colours of the fabrics you intend using. Mark the fabrics so that you know which fabric represents which colour block.
● Divide the quilt into quarters. You will notice that in the centre there is an extra row over the length and width which separates the quarters.
● Make four rectangles, of which two are similar and two are their mirror image. Stitch the centre rows separately. Join again to form the complete quilt. This quilt has 27 blocks over the width and 55 blocks over the length. The size of each block is 3,2 cm (1¼ in.) x 3,2 cm (1¼ in.).
● Cut out border strips with a total width of 16 cm (6 in.) and join around the outer edges.
● Place the top layer on the batting and the backing. Tack.
● Quilt as you wish.
● Cut out a 5 cm (2 in.) wide edge finishing strip.
● Place the strip with right sides facing against the raw edge of the quilt and stitch through all the layers.
● Fold in a 6 mm (¼ in.) hem, then fold half of the fabric strip over.
● Stitch to the back with tiny hemming stitches.

Broderie perse wall quilt with flowers, Strip-pieced blind and Spiral Log Cabin quilt

For the Log Cabin quilt, fabric colours are used so that curves are formed. It begins with a small spiral in the centre which radiates outwards.

It is an interesting variation on the usual Log Cabin quilt.

The blind is joined according to the strip-pieced method. Fabric strips of various widths are joined, cut to form triangles and then joined to form squares. The pattern is suitable for a bed or wall quilt as well.

The Broderie perse wall quilt is made of fabric with large flower motifs. The beautiful hand quilting will enhance any room.

Broderie perse wall quilt with flowers

TECHNIQUES: blanket stitch appliqué; embroidery; hand quilting; general

Size of wall quilt when completed 92 cm (36 in.) x 92 cm (36 in.)

MATERIALS
fabric with large flower motifs
90 cm (1 yd) x 90 cm (1 yd) background fabric
94 cm (1⅓ yd) x 94 cm (1⅓ yd) backing fabric
20 cm (¼ yd) x 1 m (¼ yd) fabric for binding
94 cm (1⅓ yd) x 94 cm (1⅓ yd) batting

● Follow the instructions for the broderie perse method on page 21 and stitch the cut-out flowers to the background fabric with blanket stitches.
● Draw the quilt motif on the background fabric. The quilting patterns used here are straight lines about 1,5 cm (½ in.) apart. Some of the lines cross other lines to form squares. Flowers and twigs are quilted around the edge. Quilting stitches are also applied around the appliquéd flowers, for example around the leaves and next to the twigs to enhance the flowers.
● Place the top layer on the batting and the backing.
● Begin at the centre and tack the layers in straight lines towards the outer edges.

● Begin at the centre of the quilt and quilt through all the layers. Follow the instructions for quilting on page 29.
● Once the article has been quilted, finish the edges.
● Cut out a 5 cm (2 in.) wide strip and place with right sides facing on the top layer.
● Stitch about 1 cm (½ in.) from the edge.
● Fold in a 1 cm-hem (½ in.). Fold the fabric strip over and stitch to the back with tiny hemming stitches. (Any of the other edge finishing methods may be used.)

Strip-pieced blind

TECHNIQUES: strip piecing; machine piecing; general

Size of blind is about 1,12 m (45 in.) x 1,12 m (45 in.)

MATERIALS
variety of fabrics (about 3 m)
1,5 m (1¾ yd) backing
nylon cord
strip of Velcro

Choose your fabric for this blind with care. Choose the two colours you wish to use, for example burgundy and green. You will need at least five different fabrics of each colour and the colour values must vary from light to dark.

● Begin with the burgundy fabric and cut it in strips varying from 3 cm (1¼ in.) to 5 cm (2 in.).
● Join the fabric strips to form one 14 cm (5¾ in.) wide strip. Begin with the lightest colour and end with the darkest colour. (You will need about 7 pieced strips for each colour. The strips are as long as the width of the fabric.)
● Repeat this process with the green fabric.
● Cut the joined fabric strips into right-angled triangles. You will notice that the triangles appear light or dark. The triangle where the longest fabric strip

is a light colour will appear light and the triangle where the longest fabric strip is dark will appear dark.

● Stitch one green triangle to one burgundy triangle to form a 12,5 cm (5 in.) x 12,5 cm (5 in.) square. The seams of the strips of the triangles will not correspond because the strips have not all been cut the same width. It is precisely this characteristic which makes the blocks so interesting. For light-coloured blocks, for example, join a pale burgundy triangle and a pale green triangle. For darker blocks, join a deep burgundy and a deep green triangle.

● Decide how you wish to arrange your light and dark parts, then join the blocks accordingly. (Use the photograph as a guide.) This blind begins with nine dark blocks in the centre. This is followed by sashing with light blocks all around. Next you have a 2 cm (1 in.) frame. After the frame there is another row of light blocks, ending with a row of dark blocks.

● Place the top layer on the backing with right sides facing and stitch the bottom edge. Turn right side out and pin the two layers neatly.

● The lower tube for the dowel is made about 15 cm (6 in.) from the bottom. Measure the width of the dowel and stitch two rows sufficiently far apart for the dowel to pass through. Measure the required distance between folds (about 20 cm [8 in.] to 40 cm [16 in.]) and make marks at that distance over the length of the blind. Stitch over the length through both layers of fabric. Insert more dowels if preferred.

● Stitch the side seams, taking care not to stitch the tubes.

● Sew rings on the stitching, about 35 cm (18 in.) apart, for drawing the cords in. (The distance is determined by dividing the width of your fabric by the number of cords you intend threading through.)

● Fold in the raw edges of the top layer and the backing at the top and stitch.

● Sew a strip of Velcro on the wrong side at the top.

● Tie the nylon cords to the bottom rings of the blind with a small knot and thread through all the rings. The blind is now ready for hanging.

Spiral Log Cabin quilt

TECHNIQUES: folded-over method; quilting; general

This quilt is an interesting variation on the usual Log Cabin pattern.

The colours in the blocks are arranged to form a spiral. To enhance the effect of the spiral, use boldly contrasting colours, such as purple, pink, peach and green.

The first squares of all the blocks are not exactly in the centre. First draw the quilt on paper and colour in the blocks to help you decide how to make the blocks and use the colours.

● Cut the fabric in 3,5 cm (1½ in.) wide strips.

● The centre blocks are 6,2 cm (2½ in.) x 6,2 cm (2½ in.), or 8,5 cm (3½ in.) x 8,5 cm (3½ in.).

● Draw each block on paper and colour it in. Stitch the fabric onto the paper as you would a Log Cabin block (page 15). Just remember to use the different coloured fabrics as you coloured them in. It might even be necessary to join two or three coloured fabrics to form one strip.

● Complete the top layer. Remove the paper.

● Cut out a 22 cm (9 in.) wide border strip and join it around the top layer.

● Place the top layer with right side up on the batting and the backing. Tack securely.

● Machine quilt or hand quilt through all the layers.

● Fold in a 6 mm (¼ in.) hem in the fabric of the border strip and fold over a 2 cm (1 in.) edge. Stitch to the back with tiny hem stitches.

Spiral Log Cabin quilt			
	Single	Double	King-size
Approximate size when completed	1,5 m x 2 m (60 in. x 80 in.)	2 m x 2 m (80 in. x 80 in.)	2,4 m x 2,4 m (96 in. x 96 in.)
Layout of blocks	3 x 4	4 x 4	5 x 5
Total number of blocks	12	16	25
Size of blocks about 40 cm (16 in.) x 40 cm (16 in.)			
Materials			
variety of fabric remnants	5,8 m (6¾ yds)	8 m (9 yds)	9,5 m (10½ yds)
fabric for border strip	1,6 m (1⅞ yd)	2 m (2½ yds)	2,5 m (3 yds)
fabric for backing	4 m (4¾ yds)	4,4 m (5 yds)	5,2 m (6 yds)
batting	2,2 m (2½ yds)	4,4 m (5 yds)	5,2 m (6 yds)

TECHNIQUES: strip piecing; paper-based machine piecing; machine piecing; hand quilting; general

Size when completed for double bed about 2,3 m (92 in.) x 2,3 m (92 in.)

MATERIALS
variety of fabric remnants (about 4 m/5 yds)
3 m (3½ yds) white fabric
5 m (5¾ yds) border strip fabric
5 m (5¾ yds) backing fabric
4,2 m (5 yds) batting
pattern (pages 132, 133 and 134)

I recommend that you cut the border strips wider and add more border strips for a king-size quilt. For a three-quarter bed quilt, make the border strips narrower.

If you are using the paper-based machine method for the blocks, first complete one part of the heart (where the strips run in one direction) and then the other part. Stitch the four white corners last.

These instructions are for a double bed.

● Cut out the pattern pieces from the fabric and join the pieces to complete a block.
● Join pieces 1, 2 and 3. Join the part with the shorter strips to these. Then join the part with the longer strips to this part. Join the four white triangles to complete the block. This method is quicker.
● Complete the remaining blocks so that you have 17 altogether.
● Join one or more border strips (in this case three strips of floral, green and white fabric respectively were used) with a total width of 24,2 cm (10 in.) right around the heart in the centre, so that the block measures 77,2 cm (31 in.) x 77,2 cm (31 in.) when completed. Use the mitred corner method described on page 28 so that the pattern of the border strip runs in one continuous line.
● Follow the instructions for the paper-based method (page 18) to make the border strips with the triangles (Flying Geese pattern). There are ten rectangles, each consisting of two small and one large triangle. (You might prefer the usual single-seam machine method.)
● Cut out nine 6,2 cm (2½ in.) x 6,2 cm (2½ in.) squares and join to form a square. (Join according to the strip piecing method described on page 16 if you wish.)
● Join the strips to the four sides and the squares with the blocks in the corners to form a 107,2 cm

(43 in.) x 107,2 cm (43 in.) square.
● Join a white 8,7 cm (3½ in.) wide border strip right around.
● Join 8,7 cm (3½ in.) wide strips between the remaining blocks with hearts on them and stitch around the centre part. Use the photograph as a guide.
● Cut out a 10,2 cm (4 in.) wide strip of white fabric and join right around.
● Cut out a 14,2 cm (6 in.) wide print fabric strip and join right around the outer edge.
● Place the top layer with right sides facing on the batting and the backing.
● Tack securely and quilt the article.
● Cut out a 8,2 cm (3¼ in.) wide strip of fabric for the final edge finishing.
● Place with right sides facing against the raw edge of the quilt and stitch through all the layers.
● Fold in a 6 mm (¼ in.) hem and fold half of the fabric over. Stitch to the back with tiny hemming stitches.

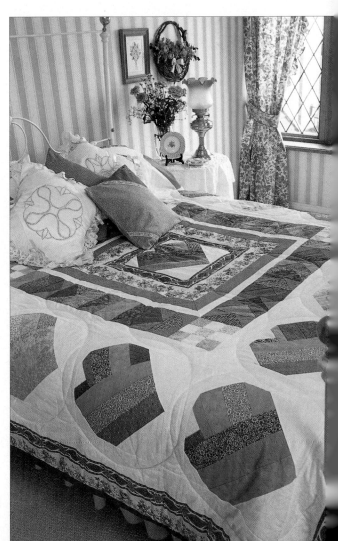

TECHNIQUES: machine patchwork; hand quilting; general

Size when completed is 92 cm (37 in.) x 92 cm (37 in.)

The centre part of the quilt forms an eight-pointed star. Around the star there are eight small 13,5 cm (5½ in.) x 13,5 cm (5½ in.) blocks which are joined according to the traditional snail's trail design. Triangles and strips are joined to this to form a large square which is placed diagonally.

Stitch the triangle and fabric strips to the diagonal sides.

Stitch a print fabric border strip around the joined fabric strips. Trim at the corners of the diagonal block.

Finish the quilt with a dark-coloured binding.

If you use a rotary cutter and long ruler, you can make this chessboard in a trice.

TECHNIQUES: strip piecing; machine quilting; general

MATERIALS
30 cm (⅜ yd) red fabric
70 cm (¾ yd) black fabric
30 cm (⅜ yd) x 70 cm (27½ in.) batting
160 cm (2 yds) ribbon, about 1 cm (½ in.) wide

● Cut four 5,7 cm (2¼ in.) wide and 45,6 cm (19 in.) long strips from both the red and the black fabric.
● Join a black strip to a red strip lengthwise. Repeat with the other strips until you have four strips, each one half red and half black.

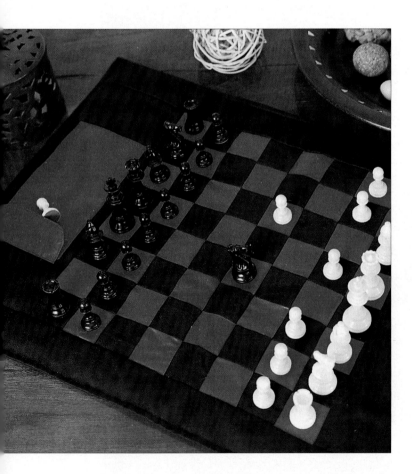

● Press the seam allowance at the back towards the black side.
● Divide each strip into eight smaller strips of 5,7 cm (2¼ in.).
● Join eight of the smaller strips so that the red and black blocks alternate. This forms the first two rows of the chessboard.
● Repeat three more times so that you have four strips for each two rows of blocks.
● Join the four strips. The chessboard part is now complete.
● Cut out two 37,2 cm (15 in.) x 15 cm (6 in.) strips of black fabric and join the strips to both sides of the chessboard.
● Cut out two 65,2 cm (26 in.) x 6,2 cm (2½ in.) strips of fabric and join to the top and bottom.
● Cut a 13 cm (5 in.) x 40 cm (16 in.) strip of red fabric for the bag. Fold the fabric in half with right sides facing. Stitch right around, leaving a small opening. Turn right side out. Stitch the opening.
● Cut out another 13 cm (5 in.) x 10 cm (4 in.) piece of fabric. Fold the fabric in half with right sides facing, so that the strip is 5 cm (2 in.) wide.
● Draw a curve on two corners away from the folded side. (Use a glass to shape the curve.)
● Stitch right around, leaving a small opening, and turn right side out. Stitch the opening.
● Stitch all around the curved corners.
● Place the part for the bag on one side of the chessboard. Stitch the two long sides and the one short side.
● Place the flap of the bag at the top and stitch. Use the photograph as a guide.
● Cut out a piece of fabric for the backing and a piece of batting, each exactly the same size as the top layer of the chessboard.
● Cut two 80 cm (32 in.) long pieces of ribbon. Fold the ribbon in half and place one piece about 10 cm (4 in.) from the top and the other piece 10 cm (4 in.) from the bottom, so that the folded part lies in the seam allowance of the top layer. Pin each one.
● Place the backing with right sides facing on the top layer and stitch right around, leaving a small opening. Turn right side out and stitch the opening.
● Quilt the article as you wish.

Amish wall hanging with cats

TECHNIQUES: machine patchwork; quilting; general

Size when completed is about 30 cm (12 in.) x 32 cm (13 in.)

MATERIALS
fabric remnants
batting
fabric for backing
pattern (page 131)

● Cut out the pattern pieces from the fabric. The quilt has six blocks with cat motifs, of which four face to the left and four face to the right. The mirror image effect is achieved by turning the templates around.
● Join pieces 1 and 2 to both sides of piece 3.

● Join piece 4 to it.
● Join pieces 5 and 6, then join to the previous part to complete the cat.
● Complete all the blocks.
● Join the blocks.
● Cut out a 2 cm (1 in.) wide green border strip and join.
● Cut out a 2 cm (1 in.) wide pink border strip and join.
● Cut out a 7 cm (3 in.) black border strip and join.
● Place the top layer on the batting and the backing. Tack.
● Quilt the cats with outline quilting and quilt on the border if preferred.
● Fold 6 mm (¼ in.) of the border strip over and fold 1 cm (½ in.) to the back. Stitch with tiny hemming stitches.

Wine bag, Fishing togbag and Beach umbrella bag

To many people, quilting means either bed quilts or wall hangings. Although men are generally not very interested in quilted articles, thinking of them as merely another kind of bed covering, they may feel rather left out if you never make anything special for them! So buy a durable fabric, such as denim or strong check fabric, and make a gift for the man in your life. Special occasions such as Father's Day or a birthday are good excuses for gifts. The fishing togbag is ideal for anglers. There is space for their hooks and sinkers, and even the reel. The fishing rod is taken apart and neatly stacked in the compartments provided. The togbag is easy to carry and can be washed when necessary.

The wine bag is a must for every household. Because it has a lining as well as batting, it will keep white wine pleasantly cool.

A beach umbrella, together with its stand, will fit neatly into the middle compartment of the beach umbrella bag. You could even make a special compartment for a light mallet if this is necessary. The umbrella bag may serve more than one purpose. When it is folded up there is space for towels and suntan lotion. Once the umbrella has been removed and the bag opened up, it serves as a picnic rug or a mat for sun-tanning on.

Wine bag

TECHNIQUES: general

MATERIALS
60 cm (¾ yd) fabric
remnants of check fabric
50 cm (½ yd) batting
45 cm (17 in.) zipper
1,5 m (2 yds) cotton tape, about 3 cm (1¼ in.) wide

● Cut out two strips of fabric and one strip of batting, each 47 cm (19 in.) x 37 cm (14½ in.) wide, for the sides of the bag.
● Place the fabric strips with right sides facing on the batting. Stitch the side seams and the top seam.
● Turn right side out.

● Stitch the raw edges at the bottom.
● Stitch the cotton tapes for the handles exactly opposite each other on both sides of the bag and equally far from the seam.
● Begin at the raw edge at the bottom and pin the cotton tape in position up to 5 cm (2 in.) from the top on the right side of the article.
● Allow about 40 cm (16 in.) for the handle and begin again about 5 cm (2 in.) from the top of the other side. Pin the cotton tape with the end ending in line with the raw edge of the fabric.
● Stitch the cotton tape securely. Be sure to make it very secure where the stitching ends at the top of the handles.
● Fold the two sides towards each other with right sides on the inside and overlapping about 1 cm (½ in.) (this now forms a tube) and stitch firmly. Do not turn right sides out.
● Cut out four strips of fabric and two strips of batting, each 10 cm (4 in.) x 18 cm (7 in.) for the flap and the base. If you wish to use check fabric for the flap, cut out one of the pieces from this fabric.
● Cut the corners to form curves. (Place a glass on the corners and draw a curve. Use this as the cutting line.)
● Place two of the pieces together with batting in between. Stitch right around the outer edge to form the piece for the base. Repeat with the other two pieces and the batting for the flap.
● Place the part for the base at the bottom of the fabric tube. Pin around the edge. (Check whether it fits neatly in the tube with the base extending equally far on both sides of the seam line of the tube.) If the two parts will not fit neatly, make small pleats to make it fit.
● Stitch neatly and turn right side out.
● Place the zipper inside the top edge of the tube. The two ends of the zipper must be at the seam of the back part.
● Unzip the zipper and stitch to one side of the tube.
● Place the part of the flap in position at the top of the tube. With right sides together pin the other side of the zipper to the flap and stitch. (It is best first to tack the zipper in order to ensure that it is neat before you stitch it.)

Fishing togbag

TECHNIQUES: machine quilting; general

MATERIALS

1,5 m (2 yds) x 45 cm (17¾ in.) fabric for the top layer
1,5 m (2 yds) x 45 cm (17¾ in.) fabric for the backing
1,5 m (2 yds) x 45 cm (17¾ in.) batting
1,5 m (2 yds) x 45 cm (17¾ in.) print fabric for the lining
60 cm (¾ yd) x 1,1 m (1½ yd) print fabric for the pockets
46 cm (½ yd) x 40 cm (15¾ in.) denim for the bag part
3 m (4 yds) ribbon or strong cotton tape, about 2 cm (¾ in.) wide
50 cm (½ yd) Velcro

● Place the backing, batting and top layer together and machine quilt in diagonal lines about 5 cm (2 in.) apart.
● Divide the ribbon in half and place them about 30 cm (12 in.) from the top and 30 cm (12 in.) from the bottom over the width of the top layer.
● Stitch the 5 cm (2 in.) ribbons from one side to 20 cm (8 in.) from the other side, leaving sufficient ribbon to tie a bow.
● Now make the bag part for the fishing rod. Take the 46 cm (18 in.) x 40 cm (16 in.) denim and make a mark halfway down on the 40 cm (16 in.) left side. Draw a line from this point to the right-hand top corner and cut along this line. Fold over a small hem in the diagonal side of the fabric piece and stitch.
● Now first stitch the small pockets to the diagonal strip of fabric.

Cut a 14 cm (5½ in.) x 40 cm (16 in.) strip of fabric for the fishing hook pocket. Fold in half with right sides facing and stitch right around, leaving a small opening. Turn right side out. Stitch the opening.
● Stitch a piece of Velcro to the top.
● Stitch the other part of the Velcro to the fabric of the flap so that it is in position for the pocket. Place the pocket in position on the diagonal strip of fabric. Stitch the two long sides and the bottom. Place the flap in position and stitch the long straight side.
● Make more pockets and flaps in the same way, using the photograph as a guide. The number and size of the pockets are your choice.
● Place the diagonal strip of fabric with right side facing on the lining. Now stitch the stitching to form the compartments for the fishing rods. Begin with 8 cm (3 in.) wide stitching and end with about 15 cm (6 in.) wide stitching. You may make the stitching even further apart.
● Fold the fabric for the flap in half over the length with wrong sides facing and place at the top of the lining.
● Place the lining on the machine-quilted fabric with wrong sides facing. Stitch right around, leaving an opening of about 30 cm (12 in.). Turn right side out. Stitch with tiny stitches. (If preferred, stitch right around the outer edge or employ any other stitching to keep the layers of fabric secure.)
● Roll up the fishing togbag and fasten the bows.
● Cut another 14 cm (5½ in.) x 14 cm (5½ in.) piece of fabric. Fold the fabric in half with right sides facing. Draw a curve on the two corners away from the folded side. (Use a glass to form the curve.) Stitch right around, leaving an opening and turn right side out. Stitch the opening.

Beach umbrella bag

TECHNIQUES: general

MATERIALS

80 cm (⅞ yd) x 1,5 m (60 in.) check fabric
1,5 m (1¾ yd) x 1,5 m (60 in.) denim
4 m (4¾ yds) cotton tape, about 3 cm (1¼ in.) wide
1 m (1⅓ yd) Velcro

● Cut a 1,4 m (56 in.) x 90 cm (36 in.) piece of denim for the outer layer.
● Stitch the cotton tape onto the outer layer for the handles. I joined the two ends of a 3,5 m (4 yds) length of cotton tape to form a circle. Then I placed the cotton tape on the outer layer to form a handle of about 90 cm (36 in.) on one side, bringing it under the bag to form another 90 cm (36 in.) handle on the other side. The tapes of the handle are about 30 cm (12 in.) from the ends of the bag. (Do not stitch the tapes right to the top – end about 5 cm [2 in.] from the top.) Stitch the tapes securely.
● Cut out two 1,4 m (56 in.) x 16 cm (6½ in.) pieces of denim.
● Cut out a 1,4 m (56 in.) x 61 cm (24 in.) piece of check fabric.
● Join the denim to both sides of the check fabric for the lining of the bag.
● Cut out a 1,1 m (44 in.) x 35 cm (13¾ in.) piece of check fabric. Fold one short side over at the top and stitch a hem. Place this fabric on the lining to form the inner bag for the umbrella. (Use the photograph as a guide.) Fold in the seam allowance of the two long sides. The short side at the bottom raw edge must be in line with the raw edge of the large piece of fabric. Stitch the two long sides.
● Place the outer layer with right sides facing on the lining. Stitch right around, leaving an opening in one side. Take care not to catch the tapes while stitching.
● Turn right side out.
● Stitch the opening.

Hot-water bottle cover and Cat cushion

Hot-water bottle cover

TECHNIQUES: machine patchwork; hand quilting; general

MATERIALS
fabric remnants
60 cm (¾ yd) fabric for back and lining
batting
piping
pattern (page 143)

● Cut out the pattern pieces from the fabric.
● Join pieces 1 and 2 to the sides of piece 3.
● Join piece 4 to form a rectangle.

● Join piece 5 to the side.
● Join piece 6 to piece 7, then join to the previous strip.
● Cut out two 27 cm (10½ in.) x 8 cm (3¼ in.) strips of fabric and join to the sides.
● Cut out a 27 cm (10½ in.) x 5 cm (2 in.) strip of fabric and join it to the bottom.
● Cut out a 27 cm (10½ in.) x 12 cm (4¾ in.) strip of fabric and join it to the top.
● Draw the cat's face with a permanent marking pen.
● Place your hot-water bottle on a piece of paper that is larger than the bottle. Trace the outlines of the bottle, but add 4 cm (1½ in.) right around. Cut out this shape from the paper and use as your pattern.

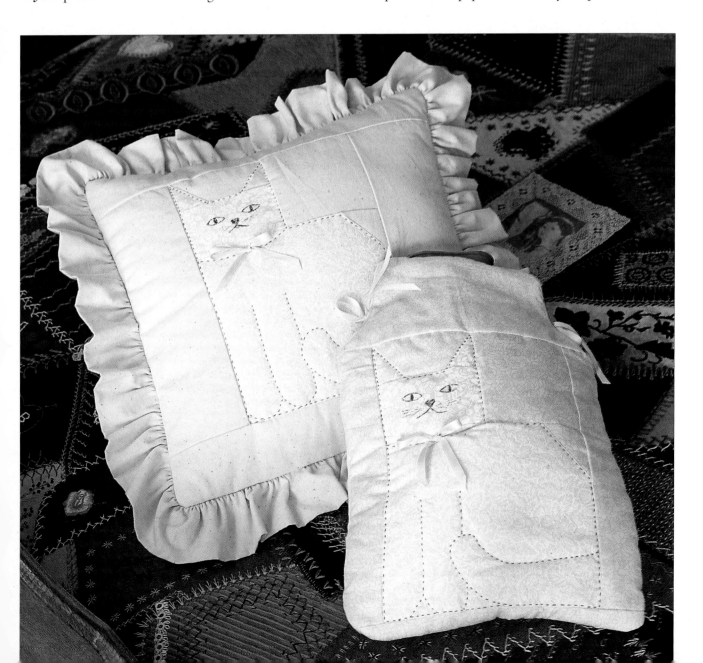

● Place the paper pattern on the joined outer layer and cut out the pattern.
● Cut out a back layer and two pieces for the lining.
● Cut out two pieces from the batting.
● Place piping all around the pieced outer layer with raw edges flush. Stitch.
● Place piping around the top edge of the back of the top piece from one side seam up to the top of the other side seam and stitch.
● Place the front side and the lining with right sides facing on the batting. Stitch to the top at the neck of the hot-water bottle. Turn right side out. (If you wish to quilt a motif, do this now.)
● Repeat with the back part.
● Place together the front part and the back part with right sides facing. Stitch the side seam from the top at the neck of the hot-water bottle to the bottom and then the other side seam. Overlock with an overlocker or finish the seam neatly.
● Tie two ribbons on both sides of the neck of the hot-water bottle so that a bow can be tied when the hot-water bottle is inside.
● Stitch a bow on the cat's neck if you wish.

Cat cushion

TECHNIQUES: machine patchwork; hand quilting; general

MATERIALS
fabric remnants
60 cm (¾ yd) fabric for the border strips and back
40 cm (½ yd) batting
40 cm (½ yd) fabric for backing
40 cm (½ yd) fabric for frill
ribbon for decoration
pattern (page 143)

● Cut out the pattern pieces from the fabric remnants.
● Join piece 1 and piece 2 to each side of piece 3.
● Join piece 4 to form a rectangle.
● Join piece 5 to rectangle.
● Join piece 6 to piece 7 and join this to the previous strip.
● Cut out two 28 cm (11 in.) x 11 cm (4½ in.) strips and join on both sides of the motif.
● Cut out two 40 cm (16 in.) x 8 cm (3⅛ in.) strips and join to the top and bottom.
● Decorate the top layer with lace and ribbon as preferred and draw the cat's face with a permanent marking pen.
● Trim the excess fabric until the top layer measures 40 cm (16 in.) x 40 cm (16 in.).
● Place the top layer on the batting and the backing. Quilt the cat with outline quilting. Quilt other motifs as well if you wish.
● Cut out a strip of fabric 10 cm (4 in.) wide and 3 m (3⅜ yds) long. Fold the fabric in half lengthwise and gather.
● Place it against the raw edges of the front of the cushion and tack.
● Cut out two 28 cm (11 in.) x 40 cm (16 in.) pieces of fabric for the backing. Sew a seam in one long side of each piece.
● Place the two parts with right sides facing on the right side of the article so that the hemmed edges overlap to form a pillow case.
● Stitch all around, finish off, and turn right side out.

HINT:
Use the pattern of the cat to make a quilt for a baby or a young child. Repeat the pattern to obtain the desired size.

Egg basket and Chicken wall hanging for the kitchen

Chickens are a popular theme for kitchens. Complement the decor of a kitchen with a beautiful chicken wall hanging. The chicken is sewn according to the inlay method and the border strip with paper-based machine patchwork. The chicken cover, which is pulled over a round egg basket, may even serve as a tea cosy. The colours of the chicken do not have to be realistic; make them to match the colour scheme in the kitchen.

Chicken wall hanging

TECHNIQUES: inlay method; paper-based machine piecing; quilting; general

MATERIALS
variety of fabric remnants in different colours
60 cm (¾ yd) fabric for the backing
60 cm (¾ yd) batting
pattern (page 136)

● The chicken is stitched according to the inlay method.
● Trace the pattern twice. One pattern is kept intact and the other pattern is cut up.
● Number each of the pattern pieces the same on both patterns and as indicated on the pattern.
● Colour in the first pattern according to the colours you intend using.
● Cut out the pattern parts of the pattern which has not been coloured in. Write down the number on the front on the back as well, but mark them 1a, 2a, etc. so that you know that it is the wrong side.
● Place the paper pieces with right sides facing on the wrong side of the fabric. If you place them the wrong way round, you will have a mirror image of the pattern and your chicken will face the other way.
● Add a seam allowance of about 6 mm (¼ in.) and cut out the fabric pieces.
● Fold the seam allowance back and tack.
● Stitch the pieces together in the following sequence:
● Join pieces 1 to 8, and then pieces 9 to 13. Stitch the two parts together.
● Join pieces 14 and 15 and stitch to the previous part.

● Join pieces 16 to 22 and stitch to the previous part.
● Join pieces 23 to 28 and stitch to the previous part.
● Join piece 29.
● Join piece 30 to 31 and piece 32 to 33. Stitch the two parts and join to the previous patched part.
● Join piece 34 to 35 and piece 36 to 37. Join piece 38 to 39. Join the parts and then join to the previous part to complete the chicken. Now join piece 40 to complete the whole block.
● Cut out a 5,2 cm (2 in.) x 140 cm (56 in.) border strip and stitch all around the square (fig. 23).
● Make the border according to the paper-based method or by hand.
● Cut the batting and backing according to the pieced top layer.

- Place the top layer with right sides facing on the backing with the batting right at the bottom.
- Stitch a row right around through all three layers, leaving an opening. Turn right side out.
- Stitch the opening with small stitches.
- Quilt the article if preferred. Outline quilting may be applied around the chicken. Or you could quilt sun rays.

Chicken cover for an egg basket

There is an opening in the chicken's body under the wing for removing the eggs.

   This pattern may also be used to make a tea cosy. Reduce the chicken pattern with the aid of a photocopier for a small teapot.

TECHNIQUES: general

MATERIALS
80 cm (⅞ yd) fabric for the top layer and backing
20 cm (¼ yd) print fabric for the wings
thin, stiff batting
fabric remnants for the comb and beak
2 eyes made of felt
40 cm (½ yd) narrow elastic
pattern (page 137)

- Trace the pattern on a piece of paper.
- Cut out four body parts from the fabric.
- Cut out two body parts from the batting.
- Cut out four wings from the print fabric.
- Cut out two wings from the batting.
- Draw a circle with a diameter of 10 cm (4 in.) on all the parts for the body where the wings must come. Cut out.
- To make the two sides of the chicken, place the batting at the bottom with two body pieces, right sides facing, on the batting. Stitch right around the 10 cm (4 in.) opening through all three layers. Turn right side out.
- Tack or pin the outer edge flat to make it easier to handle while working with it.
- Cut out a 8 cm (3 in.) x 8 cm (3 in.) square from the fabric for the beak.
- Fold the fabric in half diagonally with right sides facing out.
- Fold it in half diagonally again, so that you have a triangle which is a quarter of the size of the square.
- Cut out a 15 cm (6 in.) x 15 cm (6 in.) square from the fabric for the comb.
- Fold the fabric double with right sides facing and stitch the two side seams. Turn right side out.
- Tack the comb to the raw edge with gathers.
- Place the comb and beak in position on one part of the body. The raw edges must be flush and the beak and comb must face inwards (the same as when a frill is joined to a cushion).
- Place the other part of the body with right sides facing on the first part.
- Stitch from the front right around to the back. (Keep the bottom open.) Turn right side out.
- Make a 12 mm (½ in.) hem at the bottom and stitch, leaving an opening for threading the elastic.
- To make the wings, place the batting at the bottom with two of the wing pieces on top with right sides facing.
- Stitch right around, leaving an opening. Turn right side out.
- Place the wings in position and stitch to the top layer. (Gathered lace may also be stitched around the outer edge of the wings, if preferred.)
- Thread the elastic through the hem at the bottom and stitch the ends.
- Place the eyes in position.
- Draw the chicken cover over a round basket with eggs.

TECHNIQUES: inlay method; hand patchwork; hand quilting; general

Size when completed about 1,5 m (60 in.) x 1,5 m (60 in.)

MATERIALS
variety of fabric remnants
background fabric
backing fabric
batting

● First draw the design for the earth on paper and colour it in. (Use the photograph as a guide.)
● Enlarge the design to the required size. Make a copy of it. Mark the pattern pieces the same on both designs. Cut out one of the designs to serve as a template.
● Follow the instructions for the inlay method (page 14) and join the pieces.
● Cut out a 1,5 m (60 in.) x 1,5 m (60 in.) square from the black fabric for the background.
● Appliqué the joined motif on the background, using one of the methods described on pages 19 to 22. (Remember to remove the paper templates first.)
● Place the top layer on the batting and the backing. Tack.
● Quilt through all three layers. (Use echo quilting on the appliqué motif if you wish.)
● Join an 8 cm (3 in.) wide border strip all around and stitch to the back.

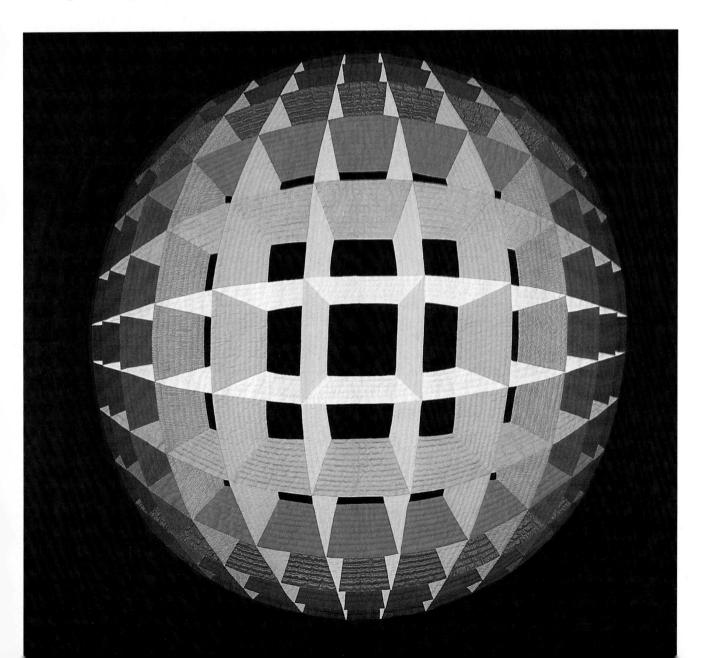

Bag for iron and Needlework holder

Both the bag for an iron and needlework holder are essential items for enthusiastic needleworkers. If you enjoy quilting while watching television, the needlework holder is ideal for placing over your favourite armchair. It holds your thread, thimble, scissors and pins neatly together.

The bag for an iron is handy when you attend quilt courses, or even when you go on holiday.

Bag for iron

TECHNIQUES: machine quilting; general

MATERIALS
50 cm (⅝ yd) plain fabric
20 cm (¼ yd) striped fabric for the handles
25 cm (⅜ yd) print fabric for the flap
68 cm (26 in.) zipper
pattern (page 137)

● Cut out two strips of fabric and one strip of batting, each measuring 72 cm (28½ in.) x 15 cm (6 in.), for the sides of the bag.
● Decorate one strip of fabric with ribbon or a strip of print fabric if preferred.
● Place the two strips with right sides facing on the batting. Stitch the two side seams and the top seam.
● Trim any excess batting and fabric at the seam allowances of the corners and turn right side out.
● Tack a row of stitching at the bottom through two layers of fabric and the batting.
● Machine quilt the strip of fabric if preferred.
● Fold the side seams towards each other. Stitch firmly with oversewing stitches, or place to overlap slightly and stitch.
● Use the pattern for the base and the flap and cut four pieces from the fabric. I used three plain fabric pieces and one print fabric piece (for the flap).
● To make the base, place one piece of batting between two fabric pieces with right sides facing and stitch a row of tacking stitches right around. (You may prefer machine quilting the base before stitching the row of tacking stitches.)

Proceed as follows to make the flap:
● Cut one strip of fabric and one strip of batting, each 72 cm (28½ in.) x 9 cm (3½ in.), for the side of the flap.
● Place the batting on the wrong side of the fabric.

Fold the strip in half with right sides facing and stitch the side seam to form a circle.
● Fold the fabric and batting in half with the batting on the inside.
● Stitch a row of stitches about 8 mm (¼ in.) from the folded edge through all the layers. (More quilt stitches may be sewn through all the layers if preferred.)
● Stitch a row of tacking stitches at the bottom along the raw edges.
● Place the batting for the flap between the print fabric piece and the plain fabric. Machine quilt. Stitch a row of tacking stitches all around the outer edge of the fabric.
● Place the sides of the flap with right sides facing on the print fabric. (The seam of the sides must be in the middle of the short straight side.) Stitch and finish the raw edges neatly.
● Pin the zipper all around the edge of the sides of the flap. Begin at the back at the side seam and stitch the zipper.
● Pin the other side of the zipper to the sides of the bottom part and stitch.
● Keeping the zipper unzipped, turn inside out and place the base inside with the outsides together. Stitch and finish the raw edges neatly.
● Cut out and join a long 1,6 m (64 in.) x 7 cm (2¾ in.) strip of fabric.
● Place the short sides together and stitch.
● Fold the strip of fabric in half over the length, with right side out.
● Fold a seam allowance over about 6 mm (¼ in.) at the raw edges and stitch. (If preferred, stitch the long sides of the handles with right sides facing. Then turn right side out and join the two ends.)
● Place the tapes around the bottom of the bag to form two equally long handles on both sides.
● Stitch the tape securely through the layers of fabric, ending about 5 cm (2 in.) from the zipper.

Needlework holder

TECHNIQUES: general

MATERIALS
50 cm (⅝ yd) plain fabric
20 cm (¼ yd) print fabric
25 cm (⅜ yd) batting
Velcro

● Cut out two 50 cm (20 in.) x 20 cm (8 in.) strips from the plain fabric and one equally long strip from the batting.

● Cut out two 20 cm (8 in.) x 20 cm (8 in.) pieces from the print fabric for one pocket.

● Cut out a 10 cm (4 in.) x 10 cm (4 in.) strip of plain fabric for the small pocket.

● Fold in a seam allowance of about 1 cm (½ in.) at the top of the small piece of fabric and stitch.

● Fold the seam allowance in at the other three sides and place on one of the print fabric pieces. Stitch the three sides to form a pocket.

● Place together the two print fabric pieces with right sides facing and stitch the top. Turn right side out.

● Place the joined print fabric on the right side of one of the long strips of fabric with raw edges together. Tack in position.

● Cut out another two 15 cm (6 in.) x 20 cm (8 in.) print fabric pieces for a smaller pocket.

● Place the fabric with right sides together and stitch one long side. Turn right side out.

● Place this joined print fabric piece at the end of the long strip of fabric with raw edges together. Tack in position to form another pocket.

● Place the two large fabric strips right sides facing on the batting. Stitch all around, leaving an opening of about 15 cm (6 in.) along one side. Trim all excess fabric and batting and turn right sides out. Stitch the opening.

● Cut out two 18 cm (7¼ in.) x 10 cm (4 in.) print fabric pieces for the pincushion.

● Place the two pieces right sides facing and stitch all around, leaving an opening. Turn right side out.

● Stuff the pincushion with batting and stitch the opening.

● Using the photograph as a guide, stitch the pincushion to the long strip of fabric to the back. (Two strips of Velcro may be stitched to the pincushion and the fabric to hold it together.)

The traycloth and coasters are made according to the folded-star method.

The fabric is folded and stitched to form star points, which are in turn arranged to form a circle. This patchwork method is very versatile. Use this method to make tablemats as well. Make circles of gold, red and green for Christmas. Attach loops to the smaller circles and use them as Christmas tree decorations. Place a folded-star circle in a card with a small window for a special occasion.

Coasters

TECHNIQUES: folded-star method; general

MATERIALS
four 6 cm (2½ in.) x 6 cm (2½ in.) squares – light print fabric
eight 6 cm (2½ in.) x 6 cm (2½ in.) squares – plain colour
eight 6 cm (2½ in.) x 6 cm (2½ in.) squares – dark print fabric
one 10 cm (4 in.) diameter circle – plain fabric
50 cm (20 in.) bias binding

● Determine the centre of the fabric circle by folding it in half twice.
● Follow the instructions for the folded-star method (page 13) up to the finishing. Proceed as follows:
● Using a pair of compasses or bread plate, draw a 10 cm (4 in.) diameter circle with a water-soluble pen over the folded star. This is the stitching line.
● Add a seam allowance of 6 mm (¼ in.) right around and trim the raw edges of the star.
● Unfold the bias binding. Tack with right sides facing and the raw edges flush all around the pen marks. Neaten the ends and stitch all around the edge.
● Fold the bias binding back and stitch with small hemming stitches.

Traycloth

TECHNIQUES: folded-star method; general

MATERIALS
four 12 cm (4¾ in.) x 12 cm (4¾ in.) squares – light print fabric
eight 12 cm (4¾ in.) x 12 cm (4¾ in.) squares – dark print fabric
three 32 cm (13 in.) diameter circles of plain fabric
one 32 cm (13 in.) diameter circle of batting
1,5 m (1¾ yd) lace

● Determine the centre of a fabric circle by folding it in half twice.
● Follow the folded-star method (page 13) up to the

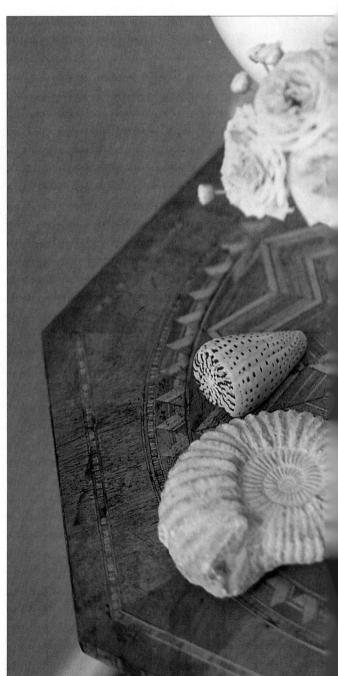

finishing. Proceed as follows:

● Use a pair of compasses or bread plate to draw a circle with a diameter of 21 cm (8¼ in.) over the folded star. This is the stitching line for stitching the frame.

● Add a 1 cm-seam allowance (½ in.) right around and trim the raw edges of the star.

● Take one plain fabric circle and cut out a circle with a diameter of 20 cm (8 in.) from the centre.

● Place the plain fabric circle and the star with right sides together so that the inner edge of the plain fabric circle is flush with the outer edge of the folded star. (The outer edge of the plain fabric circle is therefore folded back to the centre of the star.)

● Stitch 1 cm (½ in.) from the edge and fold the plain fabric circle back so that the right side faces up.

● Trim the seam allowance of the inner circle – about 6 mm (¼ in.) from the stitching line. The top is now completed.

● Gather the lace for the frill, and tack around the edge of the top with the outer edge folded back in the centre.

● Place the batting circle at the bottom, then the remaining plain circle fabric and right on top the folded-star part with right side facing down.

● Stitch right around through all the layers, leaving an opening so that you can turn the article right side out.

● Stitch the opening with small stitches.

Checkmate wall hanging

TECHNIQUES: inlay method; hand patchwork; hand quilting; general

Size when completed about 1,25 m (50 in.) x 1 m (40 in.)

MATERIALS
variety of fabric remnants
background fabric
backing fabric
batting

The use of colour is important in this quilt. The three-dimensional effect in the quilt is achieved by means of the light- and dark-coloured fabrics, as well as the quilting lines.

● First draw the design on paper and colour it in. (Use the photograph as a guide.)
● Enlarge the design to the required size and make a copy of it. Mark the pattern pieces the same on both designs. Cut out one of the designs to serve as a template.
● Follow the instructions for the inlay method (page 14) and join the pieces.
● Cut out a 10 cm (4 in.) wide framing strip and join all around.
● Place the top layer on the batting and the backing. Tack.
● Quilt through all three layers.
● Stitch a 4 cm (2 in.) wide binding around the quilt and stitch to the back.

Fan-shaped cutlery holder and Christmas angel

Fan-shaped cutlery holder

TECHNIQUES: machine quilting (optional); general

MATERIALS
1,1 m (1¼ yd) x 55 cm (22 in.) fabric for the backing
35 cm (14 in.) x 35 cm (14 in.) fabric for the pockets
55 cm (22 in.) x 55 cm (22 in.) batting
3 m (3½ yds) gold-coloured ric-rac braid
1,3 m (1½ yd) green bias binding

● Cut out a circle with a diameter of 52 cm (20 in.) for the back. Fold in half and mark the centre. Cut the circle through the centre along the line. These form the top and the bottom layers.
● Decorate the top layer with ric-rac braid.
● Cut out a circle with a diameter of 30 cm (12 in.) from the fabric for the pockets.
● Mark the centre of the circle.
● Subdivide the circle into ten equal parts and mark with a marking pen. (As you would cut a cake.)
● Make a slit in the circle from the outer edge up to the centre on one of the lines.
● Finish the edge of the circle with bias binding. Begin at the slit and stitch the bias binding all around the outer edge of the circle up to the other end of the slit.
● Unfold the circle and place the two raw edges of the slit against the straight side of the large half-circle.
● Space the rest of the small circle so that the marked parts may be pinned equally far apart onto the background to form a fan. Use the photograph as a guide.
● Stitch it to the marked lines and the raw edges.
● Place the top with right sides facing on the backing and the batting.
● Stitch right around, leaving a small opening, and turn right side out.
● Stitch the opening.
● If you wish, quilt through all the layers, or stitch along the stitching lines between the openings for the cutlery through all the layers.
● Make a pretty bow from broad ribbon and sew it on.
● Decorate the edge if you wish.

Christmas angel

TECHNIQUES: general

MATERIALS
plain fabric for the face and arms (e.g. calico)
60 cm (¾ yd) check fabric for the dress
gold-coloured fabric for the wings
1,5 m (1¾ yd) lace
2,5 m (3 yds) narrow ribbon
1,2 m (1½ yd) gold-coloured lace or decorative material
1 m (1⅓ yd) narrow elastic
golden sequins
colourless glue (e.g. Bostik)
synthetic hair
polyester filling
permanent marking pens
pattern (pages 141 and 142)

● Cut out the pattern pieces for the head and arms from the plain fabric.
● Place together the pattern pieces for the head and stitch all around, leaving an opening at the bottom of the body in order to turn right side out.
● Cut notches in the curves of the seam allowance and turn right side out.
● Stuff with polyester filling and sew up the bottom.
● Place two of the arm pieces together and stitch, leaving an opening at the top.
● Make a notch in the seam allowance of the corners and in the curves and turn right side out.
● Repeat for the other arm.
● Stuff the bottom part of the arms firmly with polyester filling. The top part must not be stuffed too much as this will make the doll's shoulders too broad.
● Stitch the opening.
● Cut out a 30 cm (12 in.) x 80 cm (32 in.) strip of fabric for the dress.
● Fold a hem in one 80 cm (32 in.) side for the bottom and stitch.
● Decorate the bottom of the dress with the lace and ribbon.
● Fold in a hem of about 1 cm (½ in.) at the top to form a tube and stitch.
● Thread narrow elastic through the tube. Measure around the doll's neck and stitch both ends of the elastic.

- Fold the dress part with right sides facing and stitch the seam.
- Place the seam in the centre at the back.
- Now make the sleeves. Make them wide so that they can be puffed out.
- Cut out two 17 cm (6¾ in.) x 30 cm (12 in.) strips of fabric for the sleeves.
- Fold each piece of fabric in half over the width and stitch the seam with right sides facing.
- Fold in a 1 cm (½ in.) hem at the top and bottom and stitch. (Leave a small opening for threading the elastic.)
- Thread elastic through the top and bottom. Pull it over the doll's head and arrange.
- Stitch the elastic.
- Push the arms through the sleeves and stitch the top of each arm to the seam allowance of the side seam of the sleeve. (The arm is slightly shorter than the sleeve so that the sleeve can puff.)
- Stitch the sleeves to the dress part, or glue it on.
- Stitch the two hands to the bottom with small, firm stitches.
- Draw the pattern for the wings on gold-coloured fabric and cut out two parts.
- Place the two parts right sides facing on batting and stitch all around, leaving an opening.

- Turn right side out.
- Sew up the opening with tiny stitches.
- Tie ribbon in the middle around the wings so that the wings are slightly pleated in the middle.
- Use the ends of the ribbon to form a loop for hanging up the angel.
- Stitch the wings to the dress.
- Attach the synthetic hair to the angel's head with glue. If synthetic hair is unobtainable, use pretty wool.
- Decorate the angel's hair with a string of sequins or any other gold-coloured decoration.
- Decorate the dress with bows as preferred.
- Draw eyes and a mouth on the face and colour in the cheeks with a little blusher.

HINT:
If preferred, place a thin piece of wire in each arm through the filling so that the arms can be bent in the right position.

Umbrella holder and Double Wedding Ring quilt

Double Wedding Ring quilt	Wall quilt	Single	Double	King-size
Size when completed	64 cm x 64 cm (26 in. x 26 in.)	1,35 m x 2,07 m (53 in. x 83 in.)	2,07 m x 2,07 m (83 in. x 83 in.)	2,61 m x 2,43 m (103 in. x 97 in.)
Layout of blocks	3 x 3	7 x 11	11 x 11	14 x 13
Total number of blocks	9	77	121	182
Materials				
print fabric – piece A	30 cm (⅜ yd)	80 cm (⅞ yd)	1,2 m (1½ yd)	1, 5 m (1¾ yd)
cream fabric – pieces B + D	50 cm (½ yd)	3 m (3½ yds)	4 m (4¾ yds)	5 m (5½ yds)
pink fabric – piece C	20 cm (¼ yd)	40 cm (½ yd)	70 cm (¾ yd)	80 cm (⅞ yd)
blue fabric – piece C	20 cm (¼ yd)	50 cm (½ yd)	70 cm (¾ yd)	80 cm (⅞ yd)
fabric for backing	70 cm (¾ yd)	3 m (3½ yds)	4,5 m (5 yds)	8 m (9 yds)
batting	70 cm (¾ yd)	2,2 m (2½ yds)	4,5 m (5 yds)	5 m (5½ yds)
bias binding, 4 cm (1½ in.) wide pattern (page 138)	5 m (5½ yds)	11 m (13 yds)	13 m (15 yds)	15 m (17 yds)

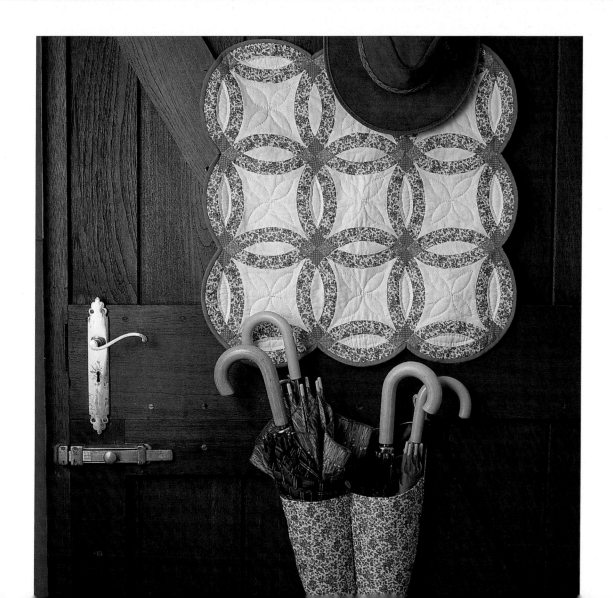

Umbrella holder

TECHNIQUES: general

MATERIALS
60 cm (¾ yd) plain fabric
50 cm (½ yd) print fabric
60 cm (¾ yd) batting
2 curtain rings

● First draw a pattern for the back on a piece of paper. Draw a 35 cm-line (13¾ in.) for the top. Draw two 55 cm (23 in.) sides diagonally to a bottom which is 18 cm (7¼ in.) long. (The sides slant towards the bottom.)
● Cut out two pieces according to this pattern from the plain fabric, and one part from the batting.
● Now draw a pattern for the front, to be made from print fabric. Draw a 50 cm (20 in.) line for the top. Draw two 40 cm (15¾ in.) long sides diagonally to a bottom which is 28 cm (11 in.) long. (The sides slant towards the bottom.)
● Cut out two pieces according to this pattern from the print fabric and one piece from the batting.
● Place the two print fabric pieces right sides facing on the batting. Stitch the top and bottom seams, leaving the sides open. Turn right side out and stitch a row of stitches at the top and bottom through all the layers.
● Take one piece for the back and place the print fabric over on the right side, about 3 cm (1¼ in.) from the bottom edge. Stitch the sides of the print fabric to the sides of the back piece. (The print fabric will puff because it is too large over the width.)
● Place the other plain fabric right sides facing and the batting right at the bottom.
● Stitch right around, leaving an opening of about 15 cm (6 in.) in one seam. Trim all the excess fabric and batting and turn right side out. Stitch the opening.
● Sew a row of stitches about 6 mm (¼ in.) from the edge right around the article.
● Mark the centre of the print fabric and stitch along the marked line through all the layers of fabric and the batting. This forms two pockets for the umbrellas.
● Sew two curtain rings at the back, on both sides at the top in the corners. (If the sunshades are too heavy, sew a third ring in the centre at the top.) Hang up the umbrella holder on the rings.

Double Wedding Ring quilt

TECHNIQUES: machine patchwork; hand quilting; general

● Cut out the pattern pieces from the fabric. First cut a few pieces of each template and test the pattern.
● To make the first circle, proceed as follows: Join piece A (also called the arc) to piece B. (First fold each piece in half to determine the centre of the curve so that you can join it neatly.)
● Join another piece A and join two pieces C (connecting corners) to both sides of piece A. The two C-pieces must be the same colour.
● Join the entire arc to the previous part to form one large disc.
● Make small marks on each of the four corners of piece D. Place the disc right sides facing on piece D and stitch up to the mark.
● Now join the second, third and fourth discs as well, so that the first circle is completed.
● From this point, join only three discs to each piece D. They fit into the previous circle. Use the photograph as a guide and complete the first row.
● Then begin the second row and repeat until the top of the quilt is completed. (With the second and subsequent rows, one piece D is initially joined to three discs, and for the rest of the row only two discs are joined to each piece D.)
● Transfer the quilting pattern onto the quilt top.
● Place the backing face down. Place the batting on top and lastly the pieced part with right side up.
● Tack securely and apply outline quilting if preferred. Quilt the transferred patterns.
● Join the bias binding right sides facing all around the edge of the quilt. Fold the bias binding over and stitch with small stitches. Where the two circles meet, fold in the bias binding so that it lies flat.

Guineafowl clock, Guineafowl table centrepiece or quilt, Miniature guineafowl wall hanging and Hanging guineafowl

Guineafowl clock

TECHNIQUES: stencilling; quilting; general

MATERIALS
50 cm (½ yd) white fabric for the front
50 cm (½ yd) fabric for the backing
50 cm (½ yd) thin batting
2,5 m (3 yds) x 20 cm (8 in.) fabric for the frill
75 cm (⅞ yd) elastic
2 m (2½ yds) broad bias binding
quilting frame with a diameter of 35 cm (13¾ in.)
cardboard circle with a diameter of 35 cm (13¾ in.)
clock mechanism with hands
pattern (page 131)

● Use the photograph as a guide and stencil the design on the background fabric.
● Place the top layer on the batting and the backing. Tack.
● Quilt the guineafowl with outline quilting. Apply any other quilting as you wish.
● Place the article in a quilting frame and make a pencil mark right around the edge at the back where the fabric extends beyond the quilting frame.
● Remove the article from the quilting frame, add a 1 cm (½ in.) seam allowance right around and trim the excess fabric.
● Stitch the two short sides of the fabric strip for the frill with right sides facing to form a circle.
● Fold the fabric for the frill in half with wrong sides facing and the two raw edges flush. Gather.
● Place the frill against the outer raw edge of the front with right sides facing and the frill folded back to the centre. Stitch.
● Place the bias binding and raw edge of the fabric together and stitch.
● Fold the bias binding over to the back and stitch. Do not stitch the two ends of the bias binding, as the elastic must be threaded through later.
● Place the article in the quilting frame to hold the fabric taut.

● Make a hole in the centre of the fabric.
● Make a hole in the centre of the cardboard circle and place in position behind the quilting frame.
● Thread the elastic through the bias binding and stitch the ends.
● Place the clock mechanism in position at the back through the hole in the cardboard and the fabric. Screw in the hands at the front.
● Paste the numbers in position on the face of the clock.

Guineafowl table centrepiece or quilt

TECHNIQUES: machine patchwork; hand quilting; folded-star method; general

Size when completed is 50 cm (20 in.) x 60 cm (24 in.)

MATERIALS
variety of fabric remnants in blue, rust-brown and green
20 cm (¼ yd) fabric for border strip
fabric for backing
batting
pattern (page 139)

Enlarge the article if preferred by making as many blocks as required and joining them. The blocks do not have to be the same size.

● Cut out the pattern pieces from the fabric.
● Join pieces 1 to 6.
● Join pieces 7 to 11 and join this to the previous part.
● Join pieces 12 to 14 and join to the previous part.
● Join pieces 15 to 18 and join to the previous part.
● Join pieces 19 to 21 and join the the previous part to complete the guineafowl.

● Repeat for the second guineafowl.
● The pattern pieces that form the background are sometimes cut longer so that it appears as if the guineafowl are at different levels. Space as preferred.
● Make folded-star points and join between the strips.

● Cut out a 9 cm (3½ in.) wide border strip and join right around the joined part.
● Place the top layer on the batting and the backing. Tack.
● Quilt the article.
● Fold the border strip over and stitch to the back with hemming stitches.

Miniature guineafowl wall hanging

TECHNIQUES: paper-based machine patchwork; hand quilting; folded-star method; general

Size of quilt when completed is 22 cm (9 in.) x 26 cm (10 in.)

MATERIALS
variety of fabric remnants in green, dark blue and rust-brown
fabric for backing
batting
pattern (page 139)

The pattern pieces for this wall hanging are tiny. They are joined according to the paper-based piecing method by machine.

I divided the pattern into strips and joined them. Then I joined the strips to complete the pattern.

With some of the blocks I added a little more green background fabric so that the blocks containing the guineafowl were not all the same size. This makes it look more natural.

● Follow the instructions for the paper-based piecing method on page 18 and complete the blocks.
● Make the points of the folded star (page 13) and join between the background strips.
● Complete the centre part of the top layer.
● Cut out a 3 cm (1¼ in.) wide strip of fabric and join it to the centre part.
● Cut out another 4 cm (1¾ in.) wide strip of fabric and join it around the previous strip.
● Place the top layer on the batting and the backing. Tack.
● Quilt the article. If you wish, embroider a row of stem stitches on the border strips.
● Fold a 6 mm (¼ in.) hem in the border strip, and fold over 1 cm (½ in.).
● Stitch to the back with hemming stitches.

Hanging guineafowl

TECHNIQUES: general

MATERIALS
variety of fabric remnants
polyester filling
bells
beads
cord
pattern (page 131)

● Trace the number of guineafowl you intend making onto the fabric (two pieces for each one). Embroider the spots on the guineafowl with French knots if preferred. Add a seam allowance right around and cut out the guineafowl.
● Fold a piece of fabric or ribbon to form the beak and the comb.
● Place together the front and back pieces of the guineafowl with wrong sides facing.
● Place the beak and comb between the two parts so that the raw edges are flush and the end of the beak and the comb point to the inside.
● Stitch all around, leaving an opening at the bottom.
● Cut notches in the seam allowance at the curves and turn right side out.
● Stuff the guineafowl with polyester filling and stitch the opening with tiny oversewing stitches.
● Stitch the guineafowl to the cord with crochet cotton or thread the crochet cotton through the guineafowl. Alternatively, thread beads and bells through to separate the guineafowl from each other. If you wish to thread a leather thong through the guineafowl, leave a small opening at the top and bottom for the thong.
● Use your imagination to decorate the guineafowl as you please.

TECHNIQUES: folded-over method; quilting; hand appliqué; general

Size when completed is 88 cm (35 in.) x 1,22 m (49 in.)

MATERIALS
variety of fabric strips (3,4 cm [1½ in.] wide) for the background (use photograph as a guide)
white fabric remnants for bird motif
fabric for border strips (20 cm [8 in.] green fabric and 30 cm [12 in.] gold-coloured fabric)
backing fabric
1,3 m (1½ yd) batting

The background consists of strips in fabric of different colours, such as blue, yellow, purple, green and brown. Some of the strips consist of two or more colours joined to achieve the right effect.

The strips are about 2,2 cm (1 in.) wide without seam allowances and the measurement for the background is about 72 cm (29 in.) x 1,06 m (42 in.).

The sun is appliquéd to the background. The bird is made and then appliquéd to the background. The bird consists of three parts: back wing, body and front wing.

● Using the photograph as a guide, draw the background pattern.

● Colour the pattern in according to the fabric colours and your own preference.
● Follow the instructions for the folded-over method on page 15 to join the background. (Remember to set aside the strips consisting of more than one colour for the time being.)
● Use the same method to join the sun part.
● Appliqué the sun on the background (page 19).
● Cut the different parts out of paper and use as templates.
● Cut out two parts of each from fabric and one part from batting.
● Place the fabric parts right sides facing on the batting. Stitch all around, leaving an opening. Turn right side out. Stitch the opening.
● Quilt the detail, such as the feathers, on the white fabric for a more realistic effect.
● Stitch the parts to the background, beginning with the back wing. Stitch the front wing.
● Cut out a green 4,2 cm (1¾ in.) wide framing strip and join.
● Cut out an 8,2 cm (3¼ in.) wide framing strip and join it to the green strip.
● Place the top layer on the batting and the backing. Tack.
● Quilt the article.
● Fold a 6 mm (¼ in.) hem in the framing strip and fold over 2 cm (½ in.). Stitch with tiny hemming stitches.

Flying Geese quilt

TECHNIQUES: machine piecing; machine quilting; general

Size when completed is about 56 cm (22 in.) x 56 cm (22 in.)
Size of blocks 18 cm (7 in.) x 18 cm (7 in.)
Number of blocks 4

MATERIALS
variety of fabric remnants
backing fabric
fabric for border strips
batting
pattern (page 140)

● Cut out the pattern pieces from the fabric.

● Follow the diagram and join the pieces forming the bird. Complete the centre block.
● Join the pieces for the eight triangles and join this to the previous part to form a square.
● Complete all four blocks and join.
● Cut out the framing strips in the following widths:
2 cm (1 in.) yellow,
3,7 cm (1½ in.) green, and
6,2 cm (2½ in.) check. Stitch in sequence.
● Cut out a 4,2 cm (1¾ in.) wide strip of green fabric for the binding and stitch around the edge.
● Place the top layer on the batting and the backing. Tack.
● Quilt the article by machine or by hand.
● Fold in 6 mm (¼ in.) at the binding and fold over a 1 cm (½ in.) hem. Stitch with tiny hemming stitches.

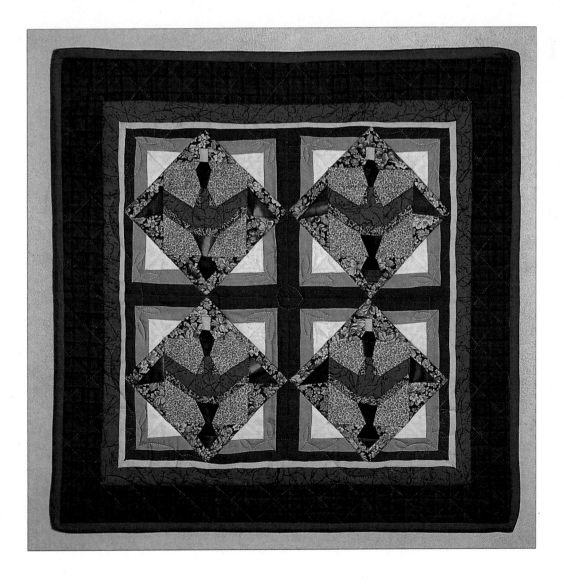

Grandmother's Flower Garden miniature quilt

TECHNIQUES: inlay method; hand quilting; general

Size when completed is 1,4 m (56 in.) x 1,4 m (56 in.)

This award-winning quilt consists of more than 4 000 hexagons. Each hexagon is about 1,5 cm (¾ in.). It was joined by hand according to the inlay method described on page 14.

The hexagons are arranged to form larger hexagons. The success of this quilt was largely a result of the use of colour. Each larger hexagon begins with a red (or darker) fabric. This is followed by a row of light-coloured hexagons, a row of medium-coloured hexagons, ending with a row of darker hexagons. The dark rows are alternated by a row of light-coloured hexagons.

The quilt was finished with fine quilting forming curves.

Christmas scene

TECHNIQUES: hand appliqué; stained-glass appliqué; quilting; embroidery; general

Size when completed is 60 cm (24 in.) x 75 cm (29½)

MATERIALS
60 cm (24 in.) background fabric
variety of fabric remnants with motifs
variety of fabric remnants
variety of bias binding remnants
sequins, beads, buttons and decorative objects
glue stick
60 cm (24 in.) backing fabric
60 cm (24 in.) batting

● Use the photograph as a guide and draw the scene on a piece of paper. Cut out the parts forming the pattern and use it for cutting out your fabric pieces.
● Glue the fabric parts you intend appliquéing onto the background with a glue stick.
● Follow the instructions for the stained-glass appliqué method (page 22) and stitch bias binding all around the raw edges, taking care to cover the ends of the bias binding neatly.
● Decorate the tree with sequins.
● Sew buttons and other decorative objects onto the

tree. Sew more buttons and decorative objects on to give the impression of standing on or in front of the fireplace.
● Sew on a star.
● Sew lace to the window to look like curtains.
● Decorate the article further as you please with whatever decorations you may have.
● Place the top layer on the batting and the backing. Tack.
● Quilt the article.
● Fold the raw edges of the top layer over and stitch to the back with hemming stitches.
● Use a pretty decorative braid to frame the article.

Christmas cloth

TECHNIQUES: folded-over method; machine appliqué; general

Size when completed is about 48 cm (19 in.) x 36 cm (15 in.)

MATERIALS
variety of fabric remnants
iron-on interfacing
backing fabric
thin batting
pattern (page 141)

● Draw the pattern for the angels on the shiny side of the iron-on interfacing. Cut out the pattern pieces and iron onto the wrong sides of the fabrics. Cut them out.
● Appliqué the design according to the machine appliqué method (page 19) on a 24,4 cm (10 in.) x 12,8 cm (5 in.) piece of plain fabric.
● Cut out ten 5 cm (2 in.) x 5 cm (2 in.) squares for the inside of the blocks. Cut out 2,5 cm (1 in.) wide strips of fabric and join around the squares according to the folded-over method (page 15). There must be three strips around each square. Complete the blocks and join all around the outer edges of the angel design.
● Place the top layer on the batting and the backing. Quilt the article.
● Cut out a 4 cm (1½ in.) wide strip of fabric for the final edge finish. Place with right sides facing against the raw edges of the article. Stitch through all the layers.
● Fold in a 6 mm (¼ in.) hem and fold half the fabric over. Stitch with tiny hemming stitches.

Christmas wall hanging

TECHNIQUES: machine patchwork; appliqué; quilting; general

Size when completed about 88 cm (35 in.) x 1 m (40 in.)

MATERIALS
variety of fabric remnants
gold-coloured fabric
backing fabric
fabric for border strips
batting
pattern (page 141)

This quilt was joined with the paper-based piecing machine method. The single-seam machine method is also suitable.

The triangles create an impression of trees. First the gold-coloured fabric is used and then different shades of green and red to create a Christmas atmosphere. If you wish, use fabrics in other colours to represent the different seasons.

● Cut out the pattern pieces from fabric. Cut 60 large triangles and 120 small triangles. There are five rows over the width and 12 rows over the length. Each block consists of one large triangle with two small triangles on both sides.

● Join the two small triangles to both sides of the large triangle to form a rectangle. Complete the rectangles and join until you have five rows with 12 rectangles in a row. Join the five rows.

● Cut out a green 3,5 cm (1½ in.) wide border strip and join right around.

● Cut out an 8 cm (3 in.) wide burgundy border strip and join right around.

● Cut out an 11 cm (4½ in.) wide print fabric border strip and join this right around.

● Cut out a star from the gold-coloured fabric and appliqué onto the background.

● Place the top layer on the batting and the backing. Tack.

● Quilt the article.

● Cut out a 3,5 cm (1½ in.) strip of fabric for the final edge finishing.

● Place it right sides facing against the raw edge of the quilt and stitch through all the layers.

● Fold in a 6 mm (¼ in.) hem and fold half the fabric over. Stitch to the back with tiny hemming stitches.

Table Mountain wall hanging

This quilt was made for a challenge competition with the theme "Festivity". The print fabric used for the outer edge of the quilt was prescribed as one of the competition rules. The other rule was that yellow fabric had to be used. I decided to make a design of Table Mountain and called my quilt "Cape Festival".

TECHNIQUES: folded-over method; machine patchwork; hand appliqué; machine appliqué; quilting; general

Size when completed about 70 cm (28 in.) x 70 cm (28 in.)

MATERIALS
variety of fabric remnants (use photograph as a
  guide)
sequins
beads
gold-coloured thread
backing fabric
batting

The fabric for the sky was yellow and I dyed some parts to create the impression of a sunset.

Table Mountain was cut from black speckled fabric and appliquéd by hand in the background.

The city lights at the foot of the mountain were made with the same print fabric used around the edge. The fabric representing the sea was from fabric which I dyed myself. Quilted lines create an effect of moving water.

In the foreground black dotted material was appliquéd. Motifs were cut from print fabric and appliquéd on the black foreground with gold-coloured thread. This makes it look like fireworks.

In the foreground on the right a tree was appliquéd so that it appears three-dimensional. The leaves were first machine-stitched with overcast stitches on the machine and then stitched to the background in such a way that they are detached from the background and give a three-dimensional effect.

This is an award-winning quilt.

TECHNIQUES: hand appliqué; embroidery; hand quilting; general

Size when completed about 1,5 m (60 in.) x 2 m (80 in.)

MATERIALS
variety of fabric remnants
white or cream-coloured fabric for the background
backing fabric
batting
embroidery thread

The motifs on this Baltimore quilt were sewn onto the background by hand with tiny stitches.

The needle-folding method (page 20) and the paper-based method (page 19) were used.

The quilt was assembled in blocks and then joined. The top layer was placed on batting and backing, and securely tacked. It was quilted by hand.

The quilt has a medallion layout consisting of a large bunch of flowers appliquéd onto the background. Bunches of grapes and vine leaves were appliquéd after this. A burgundy edge frames the block, which was placed diagonally.

Ten squares with different appliqué motifs were placed around the medallion block. Motifs such as baskets and vases of flowers, wreathes and birds were applied to the squares.

The edges were appliquéd with bunches of grapes and vine leaves before finished with a binding of burgundy fabric. Detail such as butterflies, bees, spiders and twigs were embroidered among the flowers.

The background of the quilt was quilted with diagonal lines to form diamond shapes.

Cat quilt with appliqué

TECHNIQUES: stained-glass appliqué; machine patchwork; embroidery; general

Size when completed is about 90 cm (36 in.) x 95 cm (38 in.)

MATERIALS
variety of fabric remnants
backing fabric
batting
embroidery thread
glue stick

The use of colours in this quilt is excellent. It begins with blue in the top left corner and gradually blends into a deep pink-lilac colour in the right-hand corner. This effect was achieved by joining fabric remnants. Note that all the fabrics have a dark colour value.

● Using the photograph as a guide, draw the cat pattern on the paper. Cut out the pattern pieces and use them as templates.
● Cut out the fabric pieces and place on a piece of background fabric.
● Cut bias binding and stitch over the raw edges of the motif according to the stained-glass method (page 22).
● Cut out a 5 cm (2 in.) wide strip of fabric from the blue and pink fabric respectively and stitch to the background fabric (use the photograph as a guide).
● Now cut pieces of fabric remnants into strips and triangles (join them in pairs to form rectangles) and join to form strips of about 10 cm (4 in.) wide. Stitch around the edge.
● Stitch the interesting black-and-white edge.
● Make a small square from nine blocks (Nine-Patch) and stitch a small border from the black-and-white fabric around it.
● Join more strips of fabric for a border strip and stitch this to the previous border strip. Use the photograph as a guide.
● Make the folded-star points and stitch together with the last 7 cm (2¾ in.) wide border strip. Join four squares at the corners.
● Place the top layer on the batting and the backing. Tack. Quilt the article.
● Cut out a 4 cm (1½ in.) wide strip of fabric for the final edge finishing.
● Place with right sides facing against the raw edge of the quilt. Stitch through all the layers.
● Fold in a 6 mm (¼ in.) hem and fold half the fabric over. Stitch to the back with tiny hemming stitches.

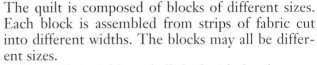

TECHNIQUES: folded-over method; machine patchwork; appliqué; quilting; embroidery; general

Size when completed about 80 cm (32 in.) x 115 cm (46 in.)

MATERIALS
variety of fabric remnants
variety of fabrics with motifs
backing fabric
batting
variety of decorative material such as beads, sequins, buttons, fabric remnants, tassels and bells

The quilt is composed of blocks of different sizes. Each block is assembled from strips of fabric cut into different widths. The blocks may all be different sizes.

The quilt is richly embellished with detail.

● Begin with a fabric strip. Join another strip to this. Continue with more strips, using the folded-over method (page 15). Make the block as large as you wish. The sizes of the blocks on the photograph vary from 29 cm (12 in.) x 29 cm (12 in.) to 27 cm (11 in.) x 28 cm (11½ in.).
● Join the blocks with sashing in between (use the photograph as a guide).
● Cut out motifs such as birds, cats, fish and flowers from the fabric and appliqué onto the background with embroidery stitches.
● If the fabrics you use for the strips have pretty motifs, you might want to outline the motifs with embroidery stitches.
● Cut out square and triangular fabric shapes and stitch onto the strip background with large stitches. The edges of these fabric shapes may also be attractively frayed.
● Stitch a small triangle onto the strip background. Use pieces of wool or loose threads of fabric for the fish tail. Sew an eye on the triangle so that it resembles a fish.
● Make folded-star points and stitch between the strips, or onto the strip background.
● Sew sequins, buttons, beads and ornamental objects onto the strip background – whatever you have at hand.
● Embroider with thin wool, crochet cotton, embroidery thread and silk ribbon on the fabric. This is a quilt which you can decorate as you wish and enjoy your creativity. Each person's quilt is unique.
● Place the completed top layer on the batting and the backing. Tack.
● Quilt the article as you wish. Again, you could quilt motifs, apply outline quilting, or whatever pleases you.
● Finish the edge using any of the methods on pages 33 to 34.

Sampler quilt

TECHNIQUES: machine patchwork; hand patchwork; quilting; general

Size when completed is 99 cm (40 in.) x 99 cm (40 in.)

MATERIALS
variety of fabric remnants
1 m (1⅓ yd) backing fabric
1 m (1⅓ yd) background fabric
50 cm (¾ yd) border strip fabric
50 cm (¾ yd) dark-blue fabric
1 m (1⅓ yd) batting

This sampler quilt consists of 13 different blocks. The size of the blocks is 15 cm (6 in.) x 15 cm (6 in.) each. (Blocks of 30 cm [12 in.] x 30 cm [12 in.] are generally used for a sampler quilt.)

● Cut patterns from the material. Use the single-seam method and complete 13 blocks with existing methods. Join the blocks diagonally (page 27), but join 3 cm (1⅓ in.) wide fabric strips in between to serve as sashing for the blocks.

● Cut out four 22 cm (9 in.) x 22 cm (9 in.) squares. Cut them diagonally so that you have eight triangles to join at the beginning and end of each row. (Except at the four corners of the quilt.)

● Cut one 25 cm (10 in.) x 25 cm (10 in.) square, then cut it diagonally twice so that you have four triangles. Join at the corners of the quilt. (You will notice that the measurements of the three triangles are slightly too large. Join in position and trim the excess fabric afterwards.)

● Cut out a light-green 3,5 cm (1½ in.) wide framing strip and join around the outer edge. Cut out a 6 cm (2½ in.) border strip from floral fabric and join.

● Place the top layer on the batting and the backing. Tack securely and quilt the article.

● Cut out a 4 cm (1½ in.) wide strip of dark-blue fabric for the final edge finishing.

● Place with right sides facing against the raw edges of the quilt. Stitch through all the layers.

● Fold in a 6 mm (¼ in.) hem and fold half the fabric over. Stitch with tiny hemming stitches.

Protea and Bushman (San) wall quilt

TECHNIQUES: hand appliqué; embroidery; machine patchwork; general

The size of the quilt is about 110 cm (44 in.) x 130 cm (52 in.)

This beautiful South African quilt was a group project undertaken by six women. It consists of a centre block on which Bushmen (San) paintings were appliquéd. The cut-away method was used, where layers of fabric are stacked one on top of the other. The top layer is cut away, the raw edges folded in, and stitched so that the bottom layer is visible. In this way thin lines (such as the arms of the Bushmen) can be stitched neatly. The framing was made according to the paper-based piecing method. It is an irregular version of the Flying Geese.

Each of the proteas were appliquéd by hand on a separate background fabric. The proteas have a three-dimensional effect as a result of the fine embroidery.

The border strip with the leaves was also made according to the cut-away technique. The guinea-fowl in the corners were appliquéd by hand and the fine detail also embroidered by hand.

TECHNIQUES: machine patchwork; general

MATERIALS
variety of fabric remnants
fabric for the backing
batting
beads
wooden animals
ornamental objects and decorative material

Since this quilt represents a painted Ndebele house, the patchwork was not done perfectly. The paint was applied irregularly, the corners are never perfect, and the lines are not perfectly straight.

● Cut out strips of fabric in different widths and join. Subdivide the strips into smaller strips.
● Pieced motifs often form a well-known object.

Join strips of fabric to represent a house, steps, and a ladder. Join curved pieces to represent the sun.
● Black and white fabric is used frequently. Blocks are framed with black fabric.
● Complete one side of the quilt and repeat more or less the same pattern for the other side.
● Stitch strips of fabric for the top part and attach the two sides to it.
● Place with right sides facing on the backing. Then place this on the batting and stitch right around, leaving an opening. Turn right side out.
● Stitch the opening.
● Quilt the article if you wish.
● Decorate with beads, ornamental objects and feathers.
● Cut designs out and appliqué it on the pieced material, using big stitches.

Pattern 1 (i)
American Jewels quilt

Pattern 1 (ii)
American Jewels quilt

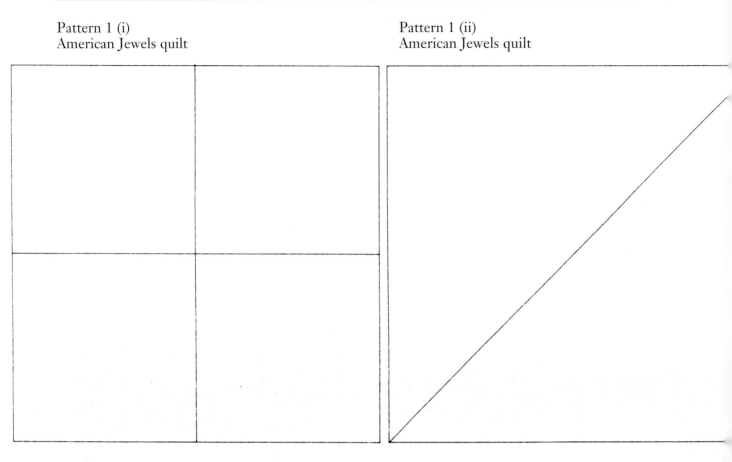

Pattern 1 (iii)
American Jewels quilt

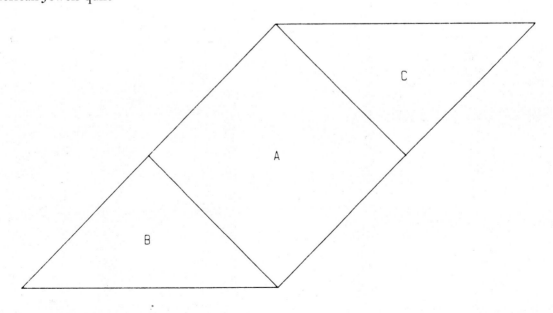

Pattern 2 (i)
Kaleidoscope quilt

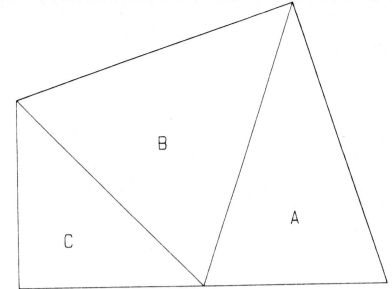

Pattern 2 (ii)
Kaleidoscope quilt

Pattern 3 (i)
Stencilled tablecloth

Pattern 3 (ii)
Stencilled tablecloth

120

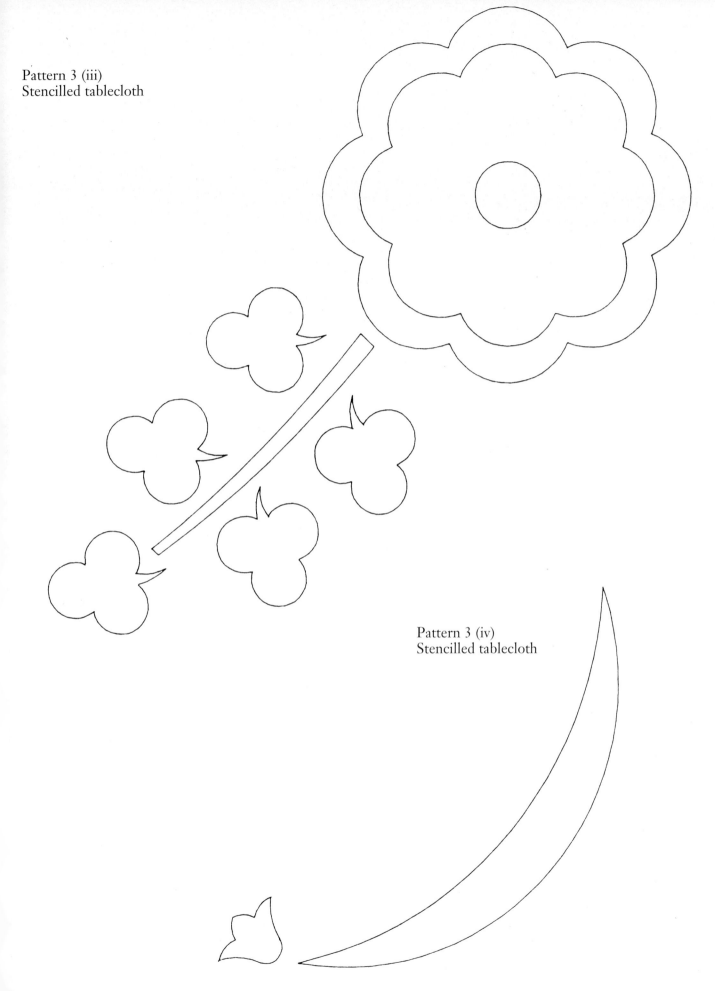

Pattern 3 (iii)
Stencilled tablecloth

Pattern 3 (iv)
Stencilled tablecloth

121

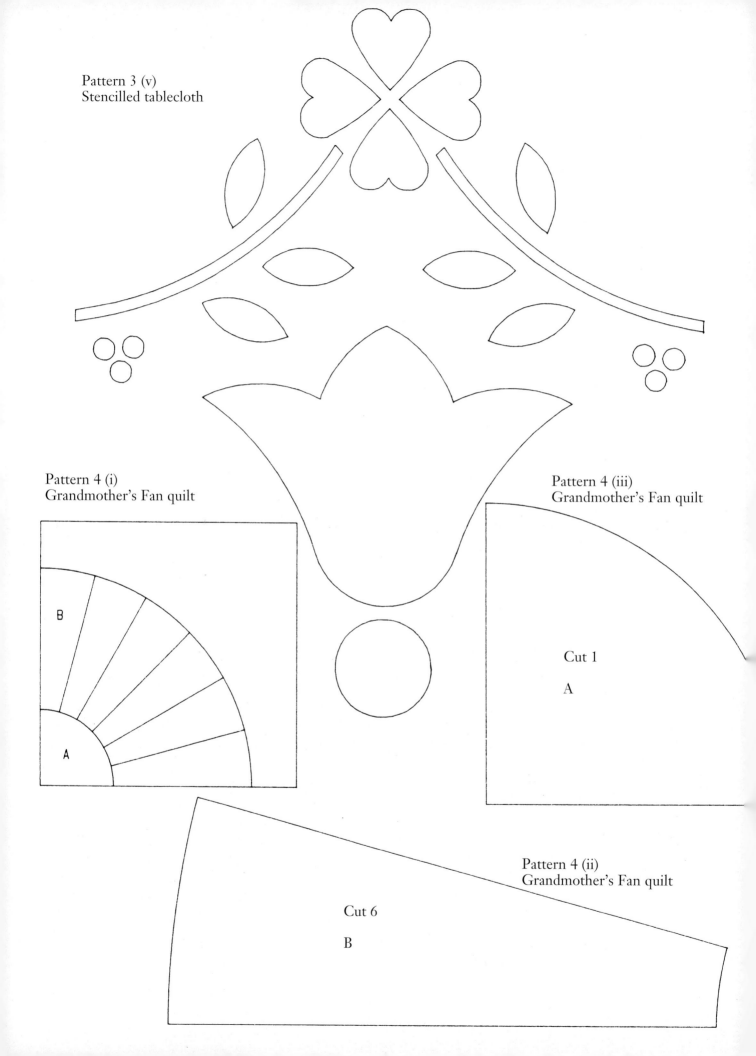

Pattern 3 (v)
Stencilled tablecloth

Pattern 4 (i)
Grandmother's Fan quilt

B

A

Pattern 4 (iii)
Grandmother's Fan quilt

Cut 1

A

Pattern 4 (ii)
Grandmother's Fan quilt

Cut 6

B

Pattern 5
Fish quilt

Pattern 7
Scrap quilt

Pattern 6
Windmill quilt

Pattern 8
Cottage wall quilt

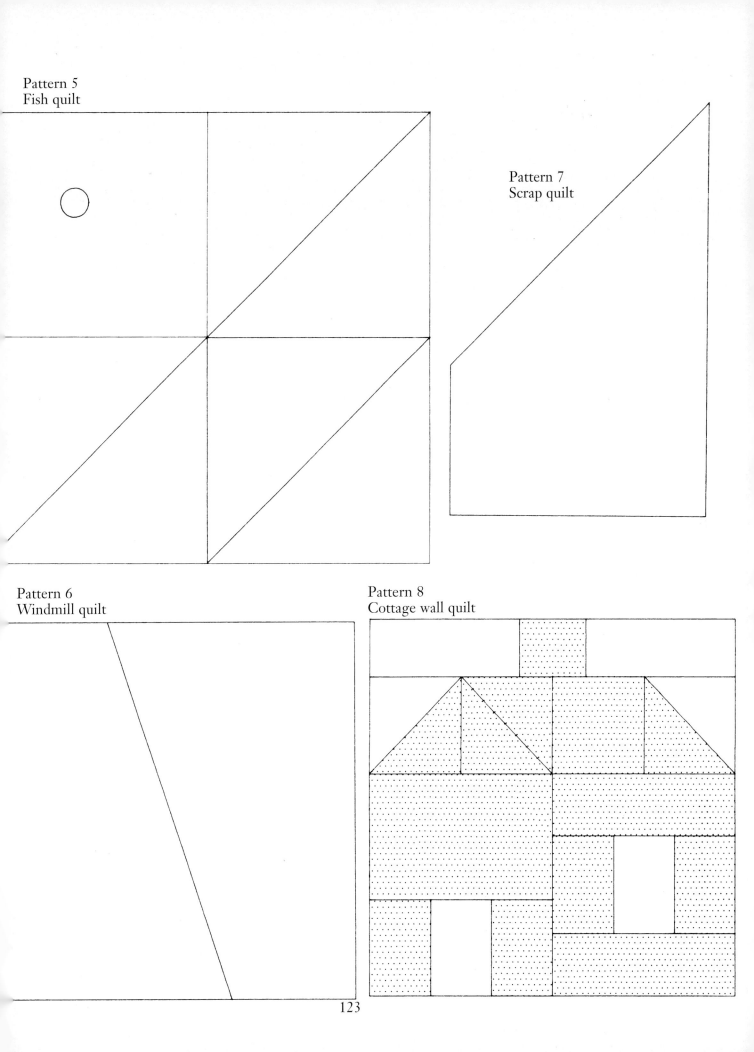

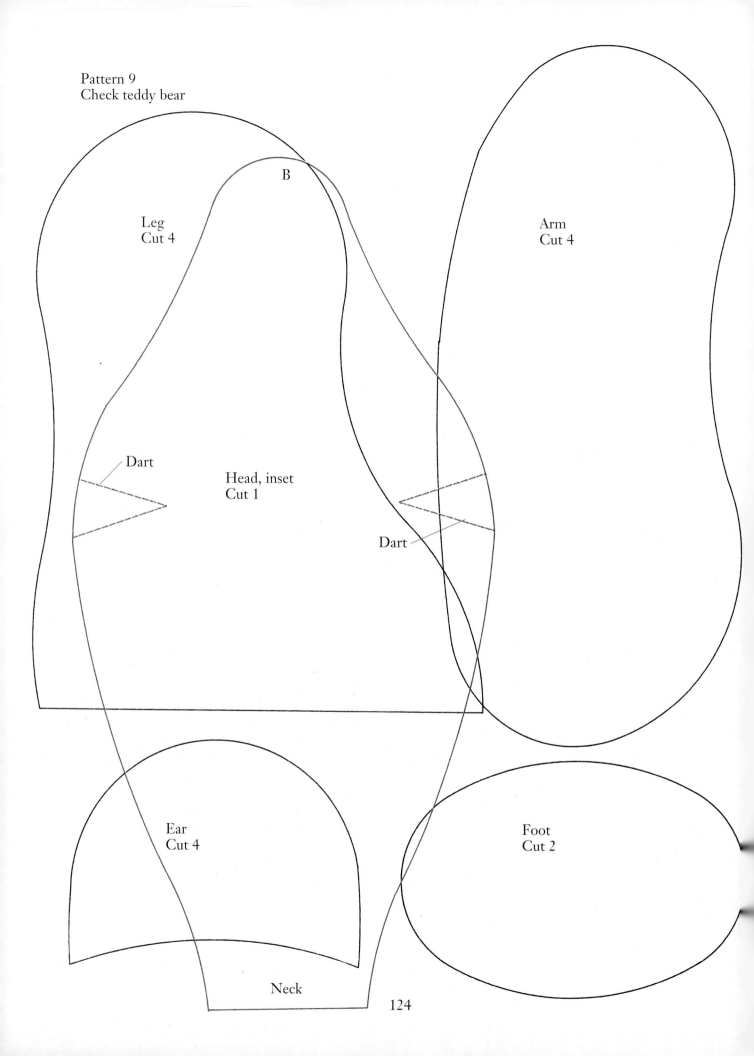

Pattern 9
Check teddy bear

Leg
Cut 4

B

Arm
Cut 4

Dart

Head, inset
Cut 1

Dart

Ear
Cut 4

Foot
Cut 2

Neck

124

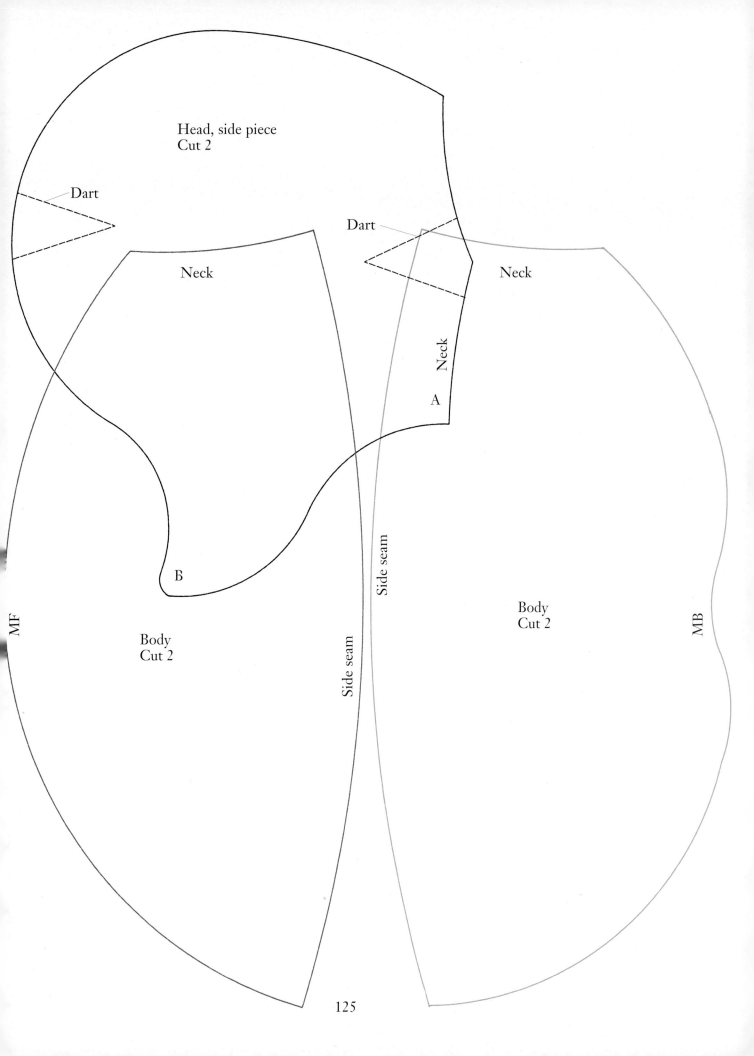

Head, side piece
Cut 2

Dart

Neck

Dart

Neck

Neck

A

B

Side seam

Side seam

MF

Body
Cut 2

Body
Cut 2

MB

125

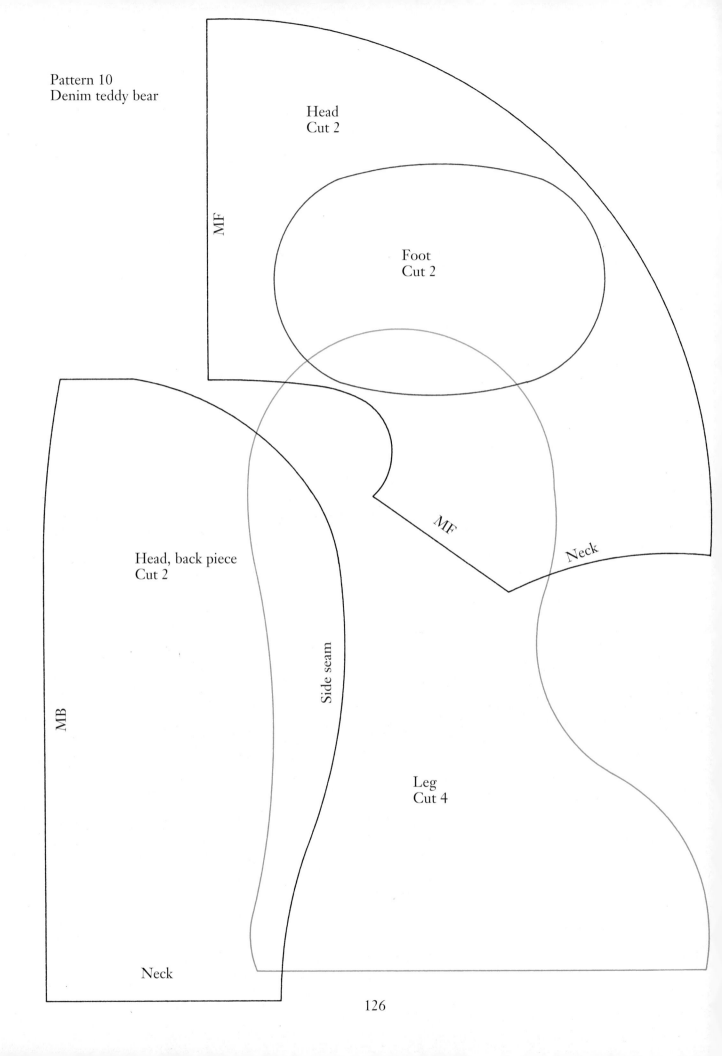

Pattern 10
Denim teddy bear

Head
Cut 2

MF

Foot
Cut 2

Head, back piece
Cut 2

MF

Neck

Side seam

MB

Leg
Cut 4

Neck

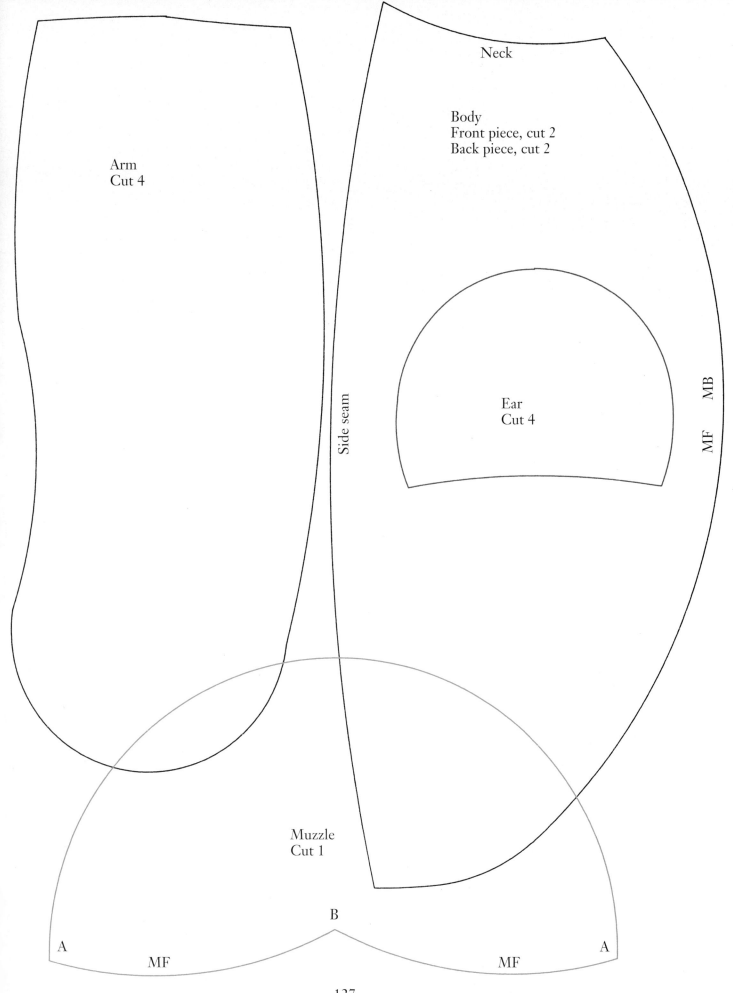

Arm
Cut 4

Neck

Body
Front piece, cut 2
Back piece, cut 2

Side seam

Ear
Cut 4

MF   MB

Muzzle
Cut 1

B

A

MF

MF

A

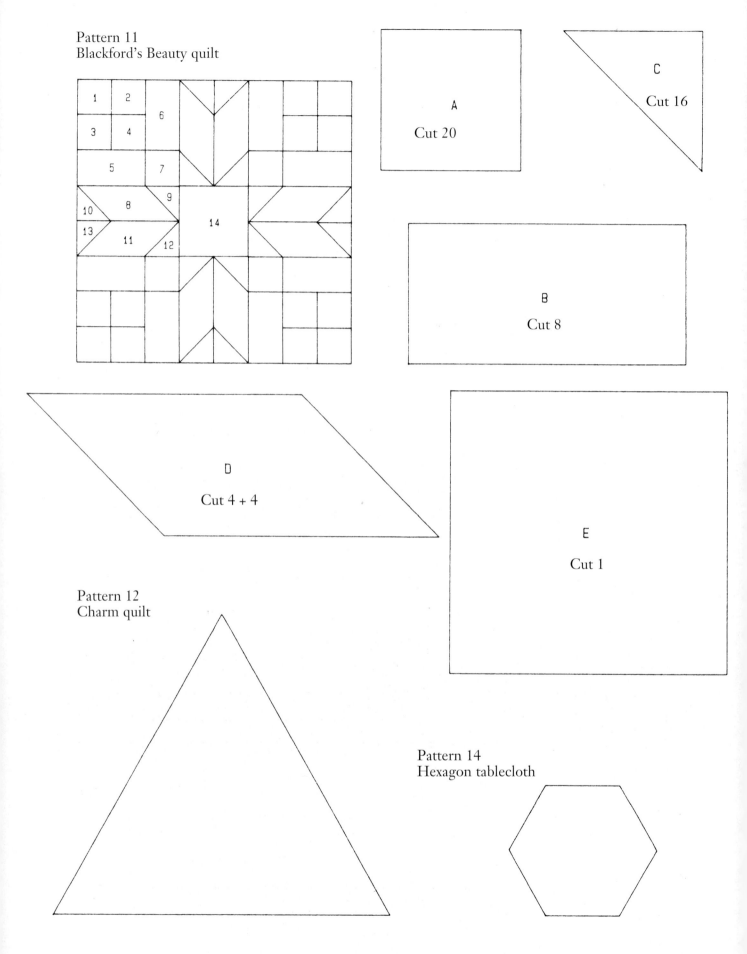

Pattern 11
Blackford's Beauty quilt

1 2
6
3 4
5 7
10 8 9
13 14
11 12

A
Cut 20

C
Cut 16

B
Cut 8

D
Cut 4 + 4

E
Cut 1

Pattern 12
Charm quilt

Pattern 14
Hexagon tablecloth

Pattern 13
Amish Grandmother's Fan wall quilt

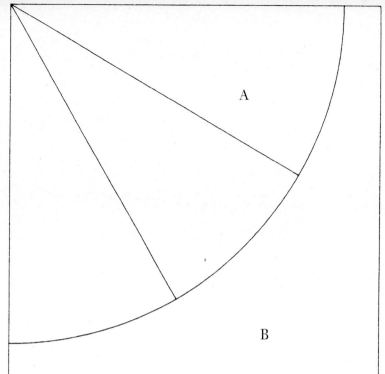

A

B

Pattern 16 (i)
Starry Path miniature quilt

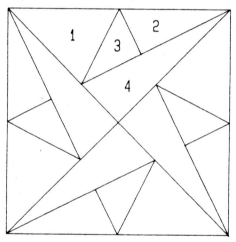

Pattern 16 (ii)
Starry Path miniature quilt

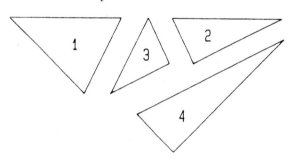

Pattern 17 (i)
Black-and-white Log Cabin quilt with stars

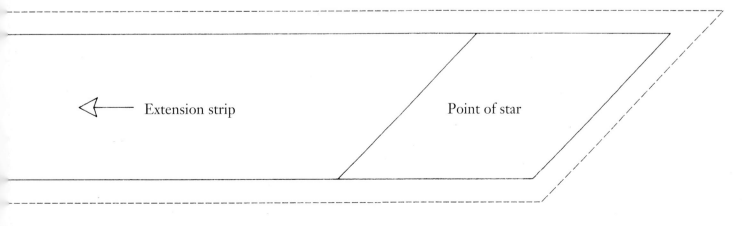

Extension strip

Point of star

Pattern 15
Postage stamp quilt

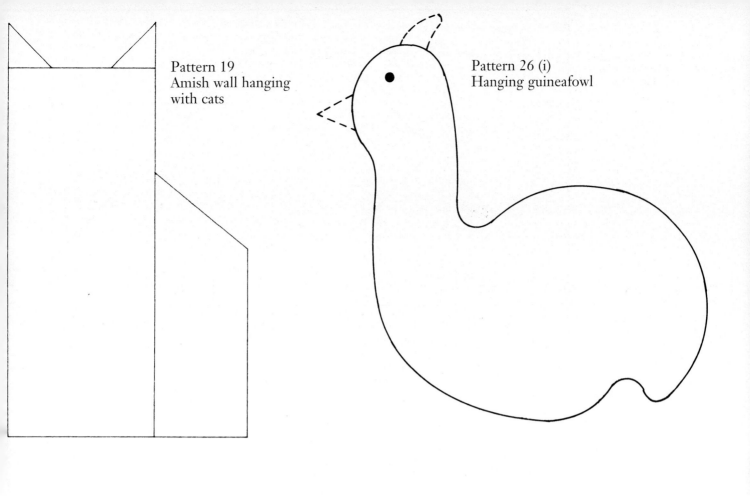

Pattern 19
Amish wall hanging
with cats

Pattern 26 (i)
Hanging guineafowl

Pattern 26 (ii)
Guineafowl clock

Pattern 18 (i)
Hearts quilt

B

B

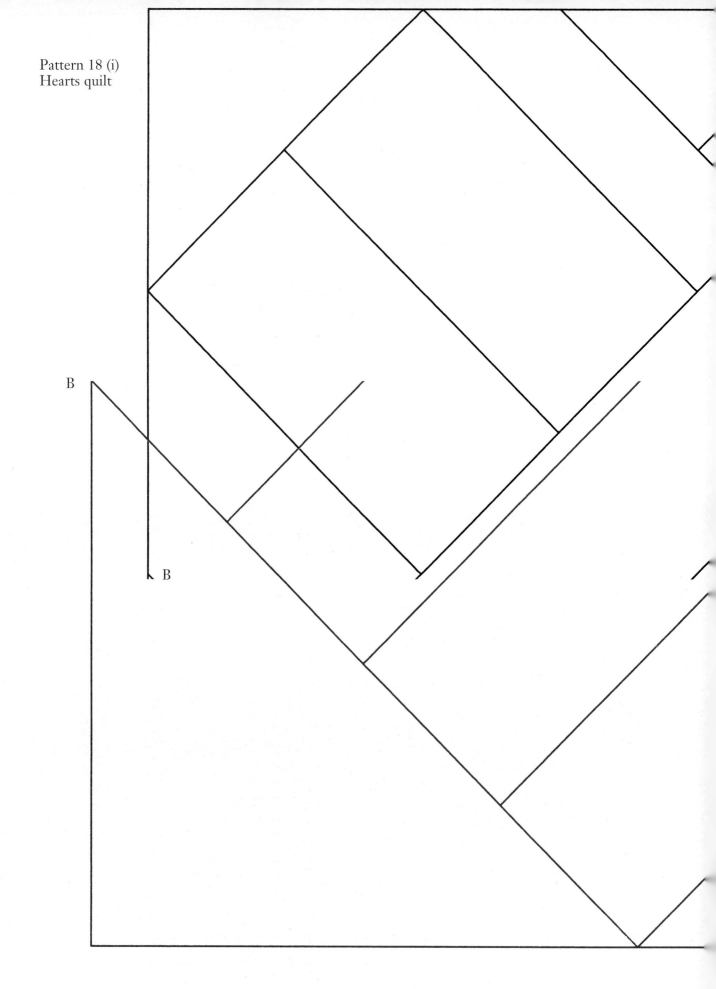

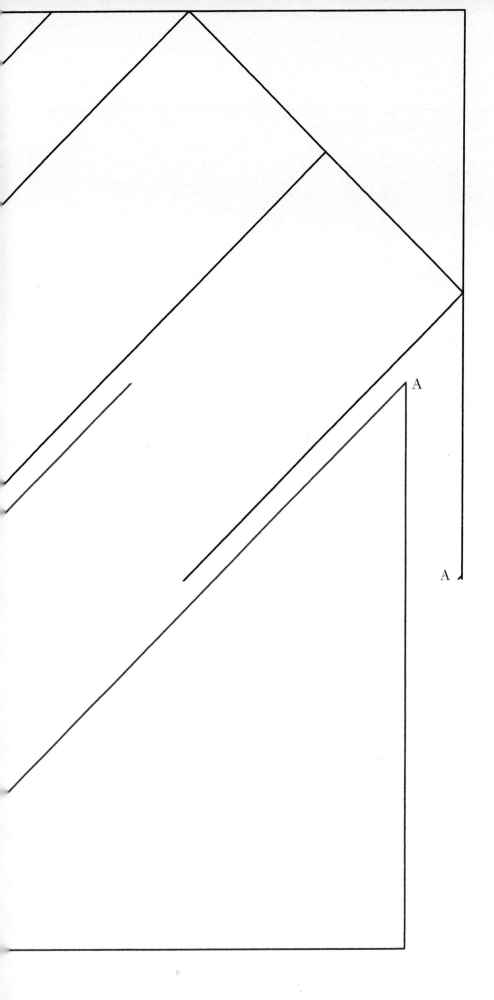

A

A

Pattern 18 (ii)
Hearts quilt

Pattern 18 (iii)
Hearts quilt

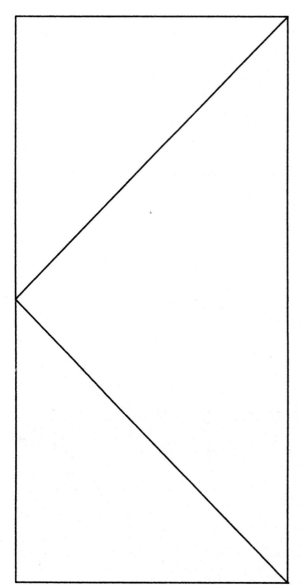

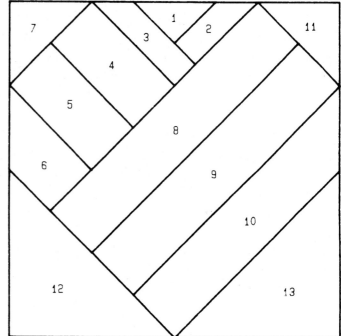

Pattern 17 (ii)
Log Cabin quilt with black block frames

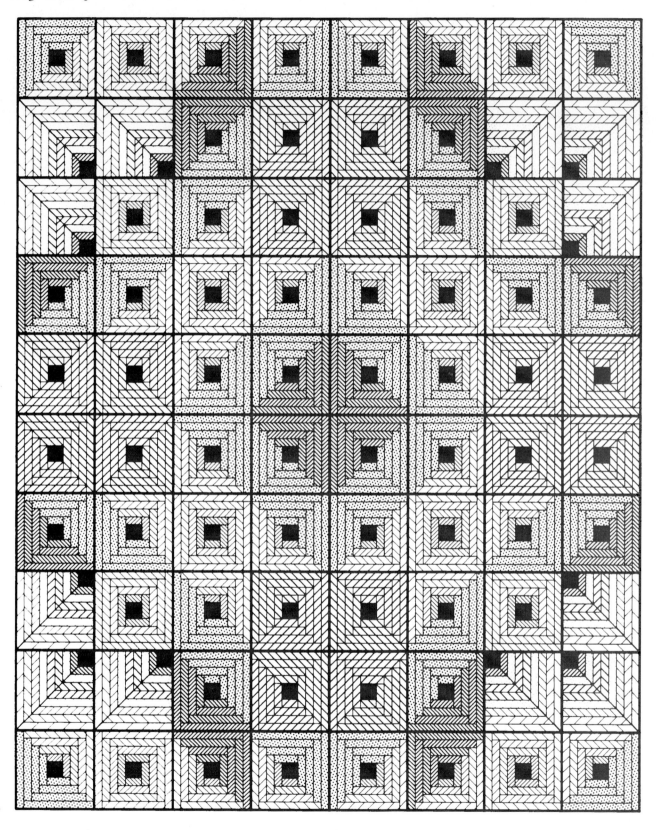

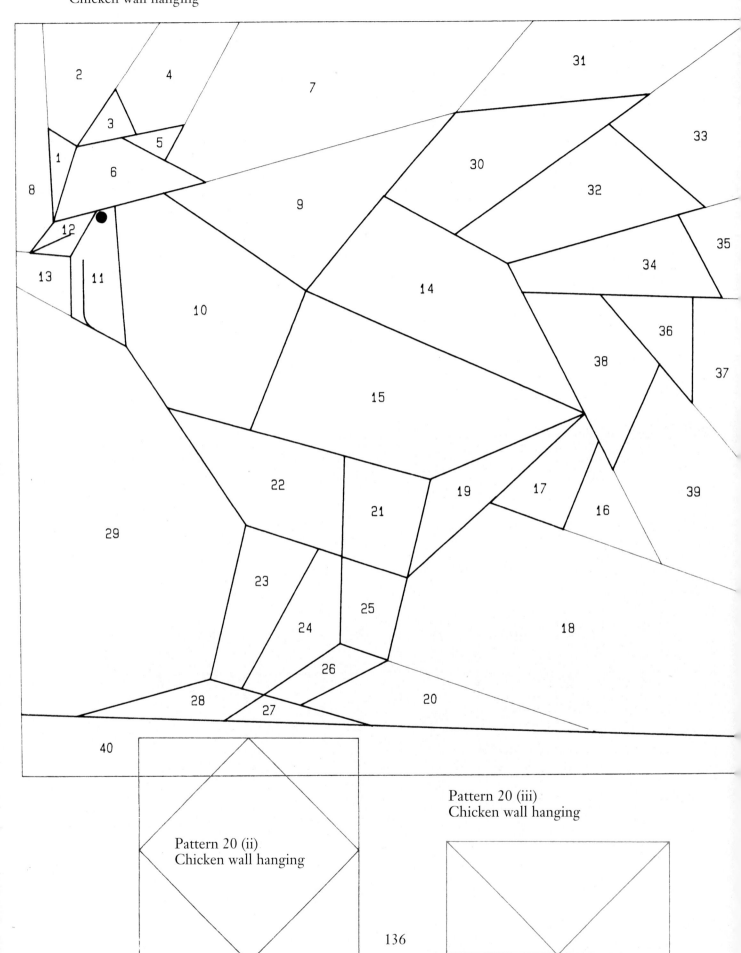

Pattern 20 (i)
Chicken wall hanging

Pattern 20 (ii)
Chicken wall hanging

Pattern 20 (iii)
Chicken wall hanging

136

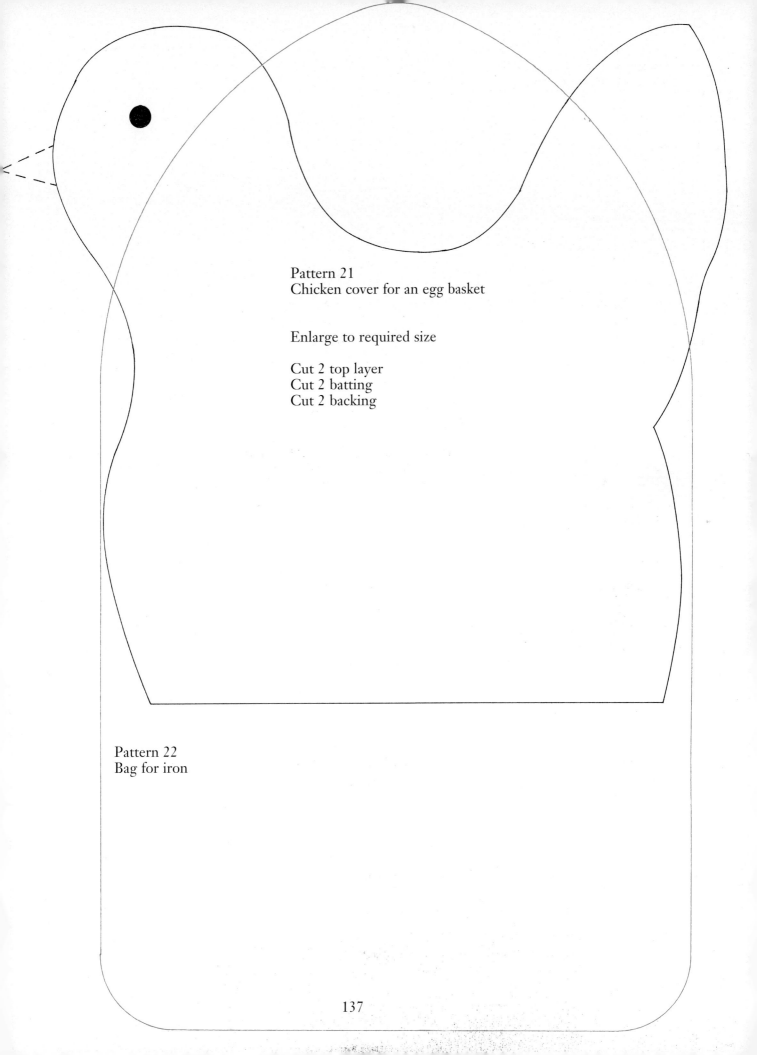

Pattern 21
Chicken cover for an egg basket

Enlarge to required size

Cut 2 top layer
Cut 2 batting
Cut 2 backing

Pattern 22
Bag for iron

Pattern 23
Double Wedding Ring quilt

B

C

A

D

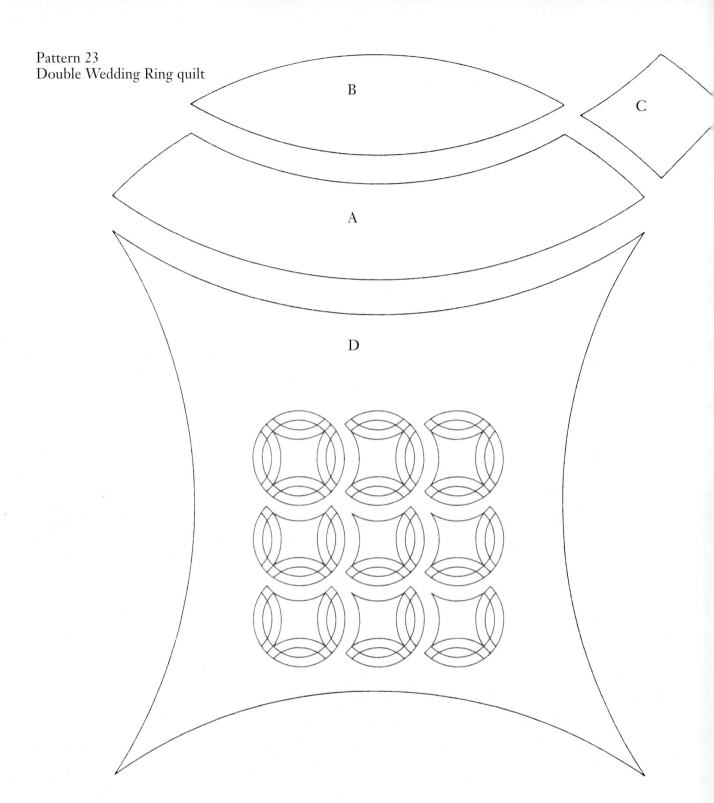

138

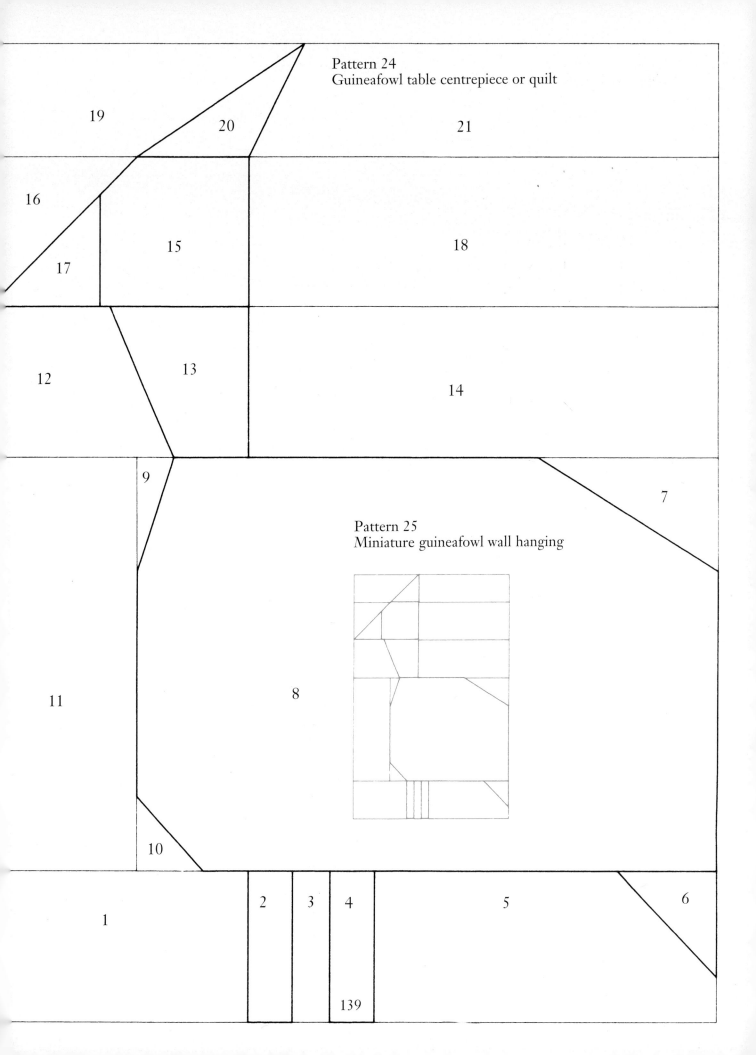

19

20 Pattern 24
Guineafowl table centrepiece or quilt

21

16

17

15

18

12

13

14

9

7

Pattern 25
Miniature guineafowl wall hanging

11

8

10

1

2 3 4 5 6

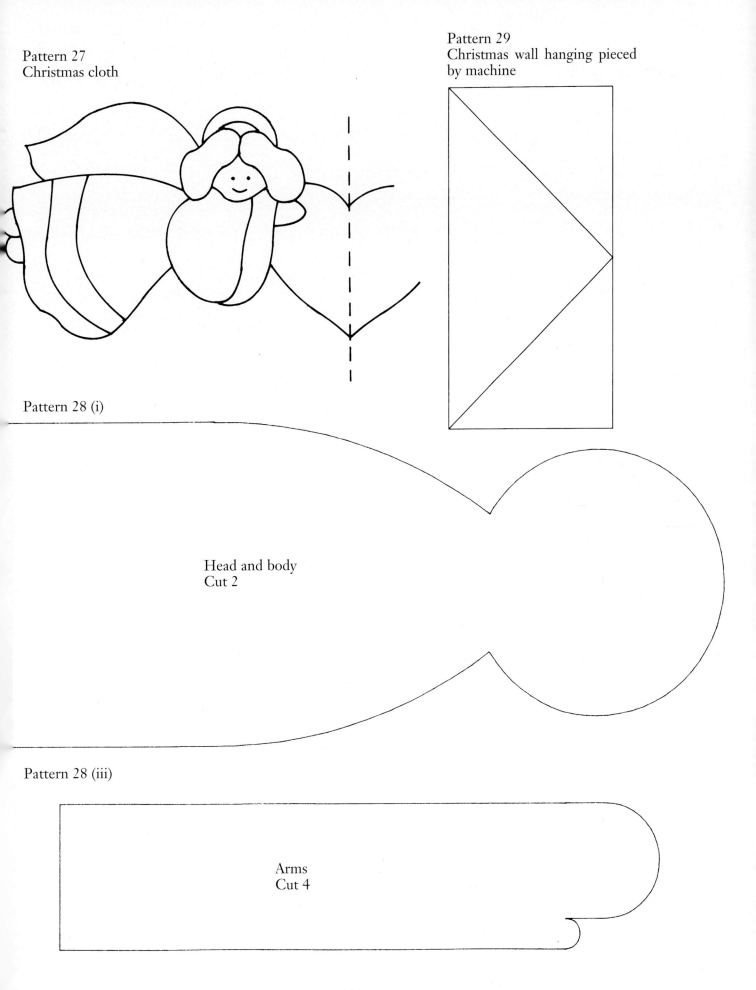

Pattern 27
Christmas cloth

Pattern 29
Christmas wall hanging pieced
by machine

Pattern 28 (i)

Head and body
Cut 2

Pattern 28 (iii)

Arms
Cut 4

Pattern 28 (ii)

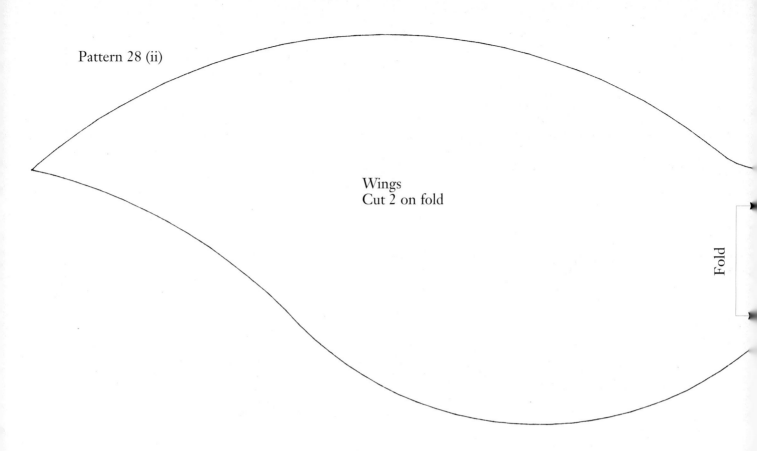

Wings
Cut 2 on fold

Fold

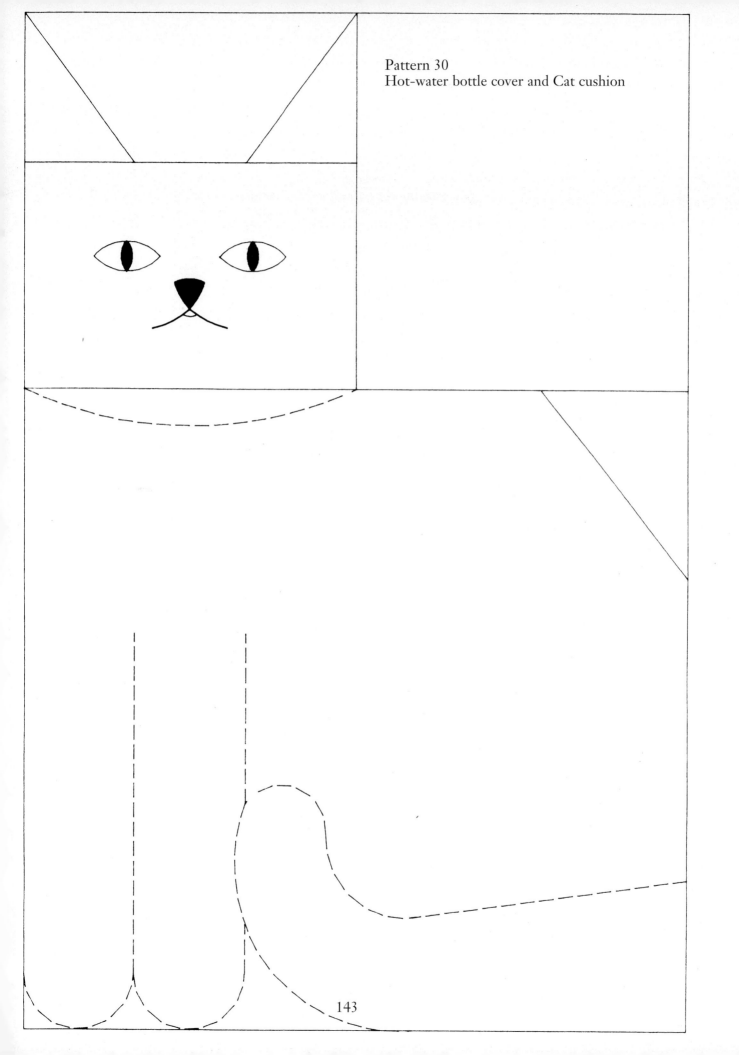

Pattern 30
Hot-water bottle cover and Cat cushion

143

Dedicated to:
My grandmother, Breggie Ziemkendorf,
and mother, Martie Groenewald.
Thank you for your love of needlework that
you also instilled in me.

All glory to God!

Acknowledgements

A book like this cannot be published without the assistance of very special people.

Firstly I want to thank my husband, Adri, for being supportive in everything I do. Thank you for the patience you, Martinette and Adriaan had while I was busy writing the book. Adri, thank you also for drawing the patterns.

The following people allowed me to invade their privacy, move furniture and rearrange accessories so that the photograhps could be taken. Thank you very much for the use of your homes: Alex and Marlene Fryer, Anthony and Lee-Ann Johnson and Fransie and Petro Streicher; I appreciate it very much.

My quilting friends were wonderful to make their articles available for the book. Thank you very much to each one: Susan Adam, Lani Bredenkamp, Estelle Cronje, Fran Davidtsz, Rita de Jager, Pam den Boester, Ansie du Toit, Suzette Ehlers, Jenny Evans, Mariëtte Fullard, Val Gardiner, Leonie Horn, Elna Lombard, Eunice Maré, Elaine Pienaar, Estelle Sieling, Susan Sittig, Cavel Stein, Jean Steward, Norma Young.

Thank you Leonie Avenant, Salomé Cilliers, Hermann Chandler, Héléne Krugmann, Jackie Niemand as well as Louis Steyn for your contribution.

A special word a thanks to Marlene Fryer, formerly from Human & Rousseau. Thank you for your inspiration while I was feeling very ill. It was a pleasure working with you over the years.

I also want to thank Nelia Richter from Human & Rousseau, Etienne van Duyker, the designer, and Anthony Johnson and Peter Bouman, the photographers for your help and patience.